The Agile Manager's Guide To

LEADERSHIP

By Walter J. Wadsworth

Velocity Business Publishing
Bristol, Vermont USA

Velocity Business Publishing publishes authoritative works of the highest quality. It is not, however, in the business of offering professional, legal, or accounting advice. Each company has its own circumstances and needs, and state and national laws may differ with respect to issues affecting you. If you need legal or other advice pertaining to your situation, secure the services of a professional.

If you'd like additional copies of this book or a catalog of books in the Agile Manager Series™, please get in touch.

- **Write us:**
  Velocity Business Publishing, Inc.
  15 Main Street
  Bristol, VT 05443 USA

- **Call us:**
  1-888-805-8600 in North America (toll-free)
  1-802-453-6669 from all other countries

- **Fax us:**
  1-802-453-2164

- **E-mail us:**
  action@agilemanager.com

- **Visit our Web site:**
  www.agilemanager.com

The Web site contains much of interest to business people—tips and techniques, business news, links to valuable sites, and instant downloads of titles in the Agile Manager Series.

Contents

Other Books in the Agile Manager Series™:

Introduction

Think of the challenges you face daily in business. You must:

- Keep customers excited about your products and services;
- Watch for competitors, who seem to spring up where you least expect them;
- Make large leaps in operating efficiencies;
- Get a handle on the complex and ambiguous markets you serve;
- Motivate workers, who are harder to mold and direct than those of the past;
- Learn and put to use, faster than ever, new procedures, practices, technologies, or regulations;
- Introduce products and services more swiftly to keep up with rivals;
- Manage change in all its variations.

Meeting these challenges demands leadership. That makes acquiring leadership skills more important than ever.

What is leadership? It's an indescribable ability—yet based on concrete principles and tools that anyone can learn—that helps you guide an organization or group of people in a beneficial direction or to a valuable destination.

The principles of leadership aren't hard to understand or apply. Anyone can be a leader. Yet the gap between leadership and ordinary management is as large as it's ever been.

That's puzzling. Who is the best motivator? A leader. Who gets the greatest effort and most insightful thinking from people? A leader. Who always meets stiff challenges and goals? A leader. Who summons from people old-fashioned workplace virtues like loyalty, commitment, and on-the-job exuberance? A leader. Who gets promoted? A leader.

So why do we have so many managers and so few leaders?

Because many believe that traditional management methods—ordering people around and "kicking butt and taking numbers" among them—get results quicker. They can, but usually at great cost in morale, personal effectiveness, and long-term success.

This book will supply the principles and tools you need to lead for the long term. You'll learn about the importance of values, mission, setting goals, good communication, symbolic action, and how to create a stable of fellow leaders around you.

It doesn't matter whether you run General Motors or a department of two. The principles are the same. And if you boss no one, the leadership techniques this book contains will do more than just prepare you for better things—it'll help you attract the attention of your superiors.

The Agile Manager's Guide to Leadership is written to go down easily. It covers the essentials of the subject in a minimum number of pages. Best, the techniques, methods, and principles will give you tools you can use on the job *today,* with excellent results.

Leadership Essentials

"A leader without a dream is a bureaucrat."

JOHN WAREHAM
IN *SECRETS OF A CORPORATE HEADHUNTER*

Chapter One

Be a Leader

The Agile Manager nodded off at his desk, which frequently happened around 2:30 P.M. His mind, freed of the burdens of the moment, traveled back to an incident that happened years ago when he was fresh out of business school and a new manager.

"Don't do it that way! What do you think is going to happen? I'll tell you—you'll melt the hose. Then who's going to buy a new one? Not me!" It was the Nasty Manager, before he grew up and became the Agile Manager. He was chewing out a maintenance worker.

"This is how we always do it," stammered the maintenance man. "Bill figured out that if you do it this way, you can save about five minutes of set-up time."

"I don't care what Bill said. And if you know what's good for you . . ."

"That's enough," said a quiet voice. It was the Agile Manager's boss, Richard Jonas.

Jonas was a portly fellow who reminded the Agile Manager of someone out of Dickens—a generous boss everybody seemed to love. He had a low opinion of Jonas; those kinds of bosses, he felt, couldn't get results.

"Come with me," Jonas said. "Carry on, Jimmy," he said to the worker. "You're doing fine."

The boss, now in his office, didn't say a word for a full minute. Then he began.

"I'm wondering whether to get rid of you right now." The Agile Manager turned white. He wasn't expecting that reaction, for one thing. For another, he hadn't thought Jonas had it in him to do it. The Agile Manager sat up, scared. "In point of fact," Jonas continued, "Bill did figure out an ingenious way to start the process without flaming the hose. It has saved this company a fair amount of money. But that's a minor point."

Jonas stared at him. "Just who gave you the power to try to hurt the spirit of a fellow human being, someone who's working hard to help you and me succeed? You were a halfback in college, I understand. Is that how you treated the guards and tackles who blocked for you? Another thing . . ."

That chewing-out lasted an hour. It was one of the most painful and humiliating experiences of his life. His rehabilitation began with an apology to Jimmy, and it continued in weekly meetings—for a year—in which Jonas filled in the education he never got in school, especially the fine art of motivating people.

But it did the trick, thought the Agile Manager as he came back to the present. In one hour, Jonas entirely reoriented my view of the work world. And was he ahead of his time or what? He "served" those he managed long before the notion became popular. And I thought he was incompetent. He was so incompetent that he became the CEO and doubled the size of the company . . .

You don't need the charisma or communication skills of former U.S. President Ronald Reagan or Sam Walton to lead. Good leaders can be quiet, gruff, friendly, imposing, shy, talkative, blustery—or any other human trait you can name, including those you have right now.

Look at Bill Gates—would you call him charismatic? Or how about one of history's great business leaders, Henry Ford? If you've ever seen a film clip of Ford, you know firsthand how hard it was for him to speak to a group of people.

A Leader Has Followers

As Peter Drucker points out, a leader is someone who has followers. Even poor leaders have followers, but usually not for long. That's because the goal of leadership is to get results. It's hard for poor leaders—who beat people up, strive to control, or pretend to have all the answers—to get anything but short-term results. Good leaders get long-term results by motivating and freeing people to focus on satisfying customers.

You don't need charisma to be a good leader. You need to stand for something.

Key to motivating people are two characteristics:

1. Leaders stand for something—ideas, values—that others respect;

2. Leaders define reality for the people who work for them (to paraphrase the insightful Max De Pree, former chairman of furniture-maker Herman Miller).

Characteristics of a Leader

Even if leaders have no common traits, they share characteristics that, in total, define their work. Leaders:

- Have the will to lead rather than manage;
- Maintain high morale among their people;
- Inspire commitment and teamwork;
- Display, at times, energy, passion, and enthusiasm;
- Are focused and able to focus those they lead;
- View the future with hope and optimism;
- Take prudent risks;
- Are honest with themselves;
- Carry on despite setbacks;
- Know their field and job in great depth;
- Work to instill values in their people;
- Orient themselves toward the customer;

- Take a long-term perspective;
- Invite input;
- Tolerate mistakes;
- Set standards and objectives;
- Remain calm under fire;
- Ensure people have resources to do the job;
- Believe in themselves and their people;
- Initiate change rather than react to it;
- Take responsibility;
- Aren't afraid to work side by side with good, ambitious people;
- Envision a better future;
- Don't blame others;
- Have a "buck stops here" attitude;
- Want to win;
- Are curious and flexible;
- Test assumptions constantly;
- Don't overcontrol;
- Give subordinates leeway to act;
- Tolerate, if not invite, dissent;
- Believe they can affect the world for the better;
- See opportunity in challenges;
- Make instinctive decisions based on experience;
- Take time to teach people their point of view.

No one will display all these characteristics. But good leaders seem to display most of them at one time or another.

Practice Leadership

You might be tempted to photocopy the list above, post it on the wall of your cubicle, and call yourself a leader.

It doesn't work that way.

You have to believe in those tenets before you can put them to use. Believing requires that you test them, reflect upon them, learn from others, and gain experience.

For instance, in preparing to write this book, I thought carefully about all the bosses I have had. Which were effective? Which weren't? Why? How could they have done better? How could I have been a better follower? The answers to those questions proved useful.

Learning to lead also takes careful analysis of your daily experiences. You can't let events breeze by you as you race off to put out the next fire. Stop and consider what has happened to you, why, what part you played in the event, and how it might have come out differently.

I remember once, as a new manager, facing an employee with a major complaint about her job. Before long, every slight she felt she'd received came tumbling out, along with buckets of tears.

Best Tip

Understand: Leadership has nothing to do with ordering people around or directing their every move.

I sat and talked with her for a couple hours, allowing her to vent on a variety of topics. I promised changes where warranted, and I followed up on them. She became a more valuable employee.

Afterwards, I reflected upon what led up to that incident and the larger event it represented. I concluded I was part of the problem—I and others rarely stopped to tell people why something needed to be done. I'd expected her to understand on her own, which is always dangerous. As a result, she had no context for her work, she wasn't sure she was doing things right, and she felt unappreciated.

The incident taught me well. I resolved to keep employees apprised of what's happening and why in any department I oversaw in the future.

Leaders Don't Over-Control

Leadership has nothing to do with ordering people around, threatening them, or micromanaging their work. A slogan that can be heard within the FedEx organization says it well: "An ounce of inspiration is worth a pound of control."

Old-fashioned command-and-control managers work a lot harder than good leaders. They need to be everywhere, solving people's problems and telling them what to do and how to do it.

Best Tip

Look ahead and make changes before they become necessary. That's a hallmark of leadership.

Good leaders, by contrast, do what's necessary to prepare people to make their own decisions and achieve goals. Then they can attend to more strategic matters, safe in the knowledge that their people are most likely doing the right thing. (And if they are not, at least they are learning.)

Anticipate and Avoid Problems

One of the foremost functions of a leader is to look ahead and make changes when called for. Even drastic changes.

Bill Gates of Microsoft apparently shut down whole programs in midstream to put people on what he considered a more pressing issue: dominating the World Wide Web. Perhaps Gates moved a tad slower than we are used to—after all, companies generally follow Microsoft, not show it where to go—but few chieftains would recommit corporate resources as swiftly or massively as did Gates.

Dress and Act the Part

Theorists deny it's necessary. Image makers and public relations people say it's a large part of the job. Cynics say it's everything.

What is "it"? The aspect of leadership concerned with outward appearances. Looking and dressing like a leader. Talking like a leader. Playing the symbolic role of a leader even if you don't feel like it.

I come down somewhere in the middle on this. If you read this book and absorb and apply its lessons, for example, it won't take much, if any, playacting to seem to be a leader. You will be one.

But you must consider your role in the context of organizational life. To motivate people properly, you may need to put on a three-piece suit. In some situations, jeans and running shoes would work better.

People won't look far beyond your grooming and clothing unless it doesn't fit the job you have. Then they will concentrate on it—instead of listening to your message.

You'll know how people want you to look and act. Satisfy them so you can get on with the job of leading.

Portrait of a Leader

A little-known leader who had a huge impact in an important event is former General William G. Pagonis, who headed the logistics operation for the allied forces in Operation Desert Storm. The work Pagonis and his men and women did in that war is widely considered one of the keys to victory.

Pagonis now heads logistics for Sears, Roebuck and is, by all accounts, doing a great job.

In the Gulf War, General Pagonis directed the thousands of people who moved men and women and matériel, fed the troops, and supplied the forward logistics bases that served combat troops.

In his memoir, *Moving Mountains*, Pagonis makes an astonishing pronouncement: During Operation Desert Storm, he didn't issue a single order.

Given the outcome of the war, that was possible only with leadership of the highest order.

Pagonis practiced many of the lessons you'll learn in the following pages. He:

- Communicated his values and the goals of the mission constantly;

- Invited input and constructive dissent from those around him;
- Offered his expertise and advice when asked;
- Managed by walking around;
- Formulated objectives (in consultation with others);
- Encouraged people to improvise to reach objectives;
- Showed respect for those who knew something he didn't;
- Worked as energetically and with as much dedication as anyone in the Gulf;
- Applied his great experience and wisdom to the task at hand.

Pagonis set the theme, trained people well, and turned them loose.

Most important, he subordinated himself to the mission. He constantly kept people's attention on it, not himself. Using power as responsibly as did Pagonis is one of the hallmarks of great leadership.

Contrast this kind of leadership with that on the other side. Under the sway of a charismatic, brutal leader, many Iraqi officers were afraid to act, fearing the consequences of personal failure. And the ground troops, coerced into serving, showed little initiative or courage when shooting broke out.

The Agile Manager's Checklist

✔ Stand for something—values, ideas, dreams—that others respect.
✔ "Define reality" for those who work for you.
✔ Keep people's attention on the organization's mission, not on you.
✔ Clothe and groom yourself in a way that fits your subordinates' idea of a leader.

Chapter Two

Start with Values

Well, of course there's speed, thought the Agile Manager, that's key, though we're lagging here a bit. He scribbled the word on his legal pad. He added integrity, innovation, always meet goals, and teamwork.

The boss had told him to come up with a list of values for the division. The boss's boss, the CEO, wanted it done because the board wanted it done. And not the whole board but that professor, who somehow swayed the rest of the group. "Just get a book and come up with some words," said his boss. "I don't really care what's on the list," he added as he headed out the door.

But I do, thought the Agile Manager. Did Thomas Jefferson go to a book and "come up with some words" when writing the Declaration of Independence?

The Agile Manager initially thought this exercise was a distraction. Now, however, he was beginning to see how promoting a set of values could perhaps shape the way people thought and acted. But he insisted on including only those values that actually moved people in the division—or should.

On the other side of the paper, the Agile Manager wrote a headline: "Values I Wish We Lived By." He started the list with the *word* meritocracy. *Too many people succeed through political wiles here, he thought. Nothing too nasty. But real. He added a corollary: No politics. Another: Get input from all levels. Ha, he thought. Often discussed, rarely seen.*

"Hey Steve" he called through the office door. His assistant came in.

"Yeah?"

"You know how consultants come in here and talk about values?"

"Sure. And it's in every business book you read."

"Well, we're joining the rest of the world. When you think about our division here, what values come to mind?"

"Off the top of my head, how about hard work, integrity, speed, and . . . uh . . . butt-kissing pays off?" Steve knew he could say that in front of his boss, who smiled. "I can come up with some more if you give me time."

"Good idea. And ask some of your friends what they think. I'll do the same and we'll see what we come up with."

The Agile Manager was happy that Steve had come up with two that he had. Maybe there's something to this after all, he thought.

Leaders stand for something—an outlook on the marketplace or how to run a business, for example. They also stand *on* something—a foundation of values.

A *value* is something considered worthy in and of itself by a person or a group. It can be a one-word standard of conduct (*respect*) or a policy everyone in a company adheres to and believes in (*we always lead in technological innovation*).

Society depends on certain values—like cooperation and honesty—to function.

Business also depends on values to function. They may be one of the noble virtues that have prevailed in all times and all places, like integrity or honor. These are what Stephen Covey calls principle-based values. Other examples include fairness, cooperation, and kindness.

Values may also be concepts considered important by a select group, and not by others. Company A, for instance, may value speed even if it means more mistakes, while Company B values getting it right the first time, no matter how long it takes.

Values may be explicitly stated, as they are more and more in organizations. Or they may be unspoken, yet recognized by all.

Among Your Most Powerful Tools

Values are extremely powerful. They form the foundation for the United States of America, for example. Values here include freedom of speech, freedom from the tyranny of a state religion, individuality, independence, and many more. Such values shape our lives and daily experiences profoundly.

Values guide people. They identify what behavior is acceptable, and what behavior is not.

Best Tip

Use values to help people understand what is desirable behavior and what isn't. They are more powerful than rules.

People may be dishonest, but dishonest people know, at some level, that their behavior is unacceptable in our society.

Be Aware of Unspoken Values

Organizations also have unspoken values that people live by but rarely talk about, except on the sly. Some polluted companies, for instance, live by values like these:

- Always cover your butt,
- Never deliver bad news,
- Blame the worker not present,
- Never contradict the boss,
- Those lower than you on the ladder are scum,
- Dishonesty is sometimes OK,
- Steal resources from other groups when you can,
- Don't make waves.

Take note of these destructive values. Leaders work to disable them, something best done by highlighting more constructive values and operating in accordance with them.

Values: Better than Rules

Forward-thinking companies promote values to guide people. Doing so saves time because the organization need not write rules, and employees need not refer to rule books or the company manual.

Retailer Nordstrom, for example, holds dear a potent value: *the customer is king.* Employees at the lowest level thus don't waste one second wondering if they should take a return without a receipt. They do it and get on with the next transaction.

Values Outlive Goals

An explicit set of values should form the foundation of any company or department, because they endure.

Disable destructive values like "Lying is sometimes OK."

Jan Carlzon, former head of Scandinavian Airlines, believes values are important because they outlive goals. If a company is purely goal oriented, it may reach a goal and then wonder what to do next. Say you have a goal to become a $25 million company. Once you reach it, what next? Should you hold steady, contract a bit, or grow? If the company, however, has a value like "Growth is good," then the next goal is easy to formulate: Get to $50 million in sales.

Values Send a Message

A good value teaches and guides any employee, even those new at the company.

A value at Steuben Glassworks: *We do flawless work.* If any piece shows a flaw, employees shatter it. That powerful, symbolic act affirms the value over and over. Employees learn immediately that they can't compromise on quality.

Values Shape an Organization

A key value at car manufacturer Saturn is *trust*. That value manifests itself in various ways. Employees, all on salary, are free to set their own working hours and vacation times. The company also dispenses with quality inspectors—it trusts employees to produce quality goods. (Saturn has good systems to help them do it.)

A key value at Corning, Inc., is *leadership*. One way the company interprets that value is this: "The goods and services we produce are never merely ordinary and must always be truly useful."

To identify your organization's values, look around. People are operating in accordance with certain ideas, whether they are published or not.

If you work in R&D or product development at Corning, that value guides what you do, hour by hour.

3M, which calls its values "Principles of Management," holds *innovation* dear: "Our first principle is the promotion of entrepreneurship and insistence upon freedom in the work place to pursue innovative ideas."

That value gives rise to such practices as 3M's "15 percent rule." It allows technical people to spend 15 percent of their work time on projects of their own choosing.

That value also helps ensure that, as managers come and go, 3M will still foster innovation through organizational practice and structure.

Finally a core value at pharmaceutical company Merck is *service to humanity*. That value guarantees that managers keep financial objectives secondary. Merck has been known to give away the drugs it makes to honor that value. (Merck, incidentally, has a stellar track record when it comes to financial results. Many of the best companies recognize that when you focus on a higher mission than making money, all the money you need follows.)

Identify Your Values

You've seen how values can shape and animate an organization. Now it's time to identify those that can propel you into better territory. Maybe your company has a list of values already. If so, be a leader and act upon them, even if other managers, including those senior to you, don't.

But most companies, especially smaller ones, haven't published their values. You'll be a better manager if you take matters into your own hands and live by values you'd like to instill in those around you. You can do this even if all you manage is the temp pool.

Be smart, though. If creating and promoting values would upset or threaten your boss, keep the list to yourself and a few others.

Here are a few guidelines:

Look around. List the values that currently hold sway in your department, both constructive and destructive. (You'll have some of both.) Many of these, if not most, will be obvious to you. If you're in doubt, investigate what kind of behavior senior managers praise, who gets promoted and for what, and what senior managers talk or write about all the time. (Loyalty? Financial results? The rights of shareholders?) And remember—a value can be a word, phrase, or sentence.

Ask for input. Ask those that work with and for you what values the organization has, as well as those they feel it needs. How do they want to be treated? How do they want to be seen by others, such as customers or vendors? If your subordinates trust you, you'll get a lot of useful information.

I once worked for an organization that espoused the value of soliciting and using input from people at all levels. But any of the lower-level workers who dared offer input once rarely did again. Not only was it not acted on, but they got the firm message, "Mind your own business!" That was the real value. Values like these may be hidden from you, yet well known to your fellow workers.

List your ideal values. Make a list of values you'd like to instill in your local culture. The list of values in key word form on the next page can give you some ideas.

Also, ask yourself: Which values do you teach your children? Which values do you wish your company had? A good value sets explicit standards for behavior, like "honesty in all we do." Or "cooperation and teamwork." These values, in addition, should harmonize with those your people already have—or should have. (If they are an independent bunch of Generation Xers, for example, you wouldn't get far trying to instill a value like "Always follow the rules.")

Best Tip

To come up with values, ask for input. "What values do we already have? Which ones do you think we need?"

Combine your values into one short list. Pick a handful of values to highlight and promote. The list shouldn't be long. Long lists repel and confuse people.

Your list can contain just one value. Corporate travel agent Rosenbluth International, for example, has a single guiding value: *Put employees first.* (CEO Hal Rosenbluth even wrote a book called *The Customer Comes Second.* The idea is that if you keep your people happy, they'll keep customers happy.)

Publish the values. Let people know your values. Put them on plaques and hang them where people will see them. Put them on laminated wallet cards. Put them in the annual report, on your Web site, and in the employee newsletter (and not just once—have them appear, with the mission, in every issue). Last, talk about the values incessantly until people understand you mean them.

Live the Values

Companies often congratulate themselves for coming up with a noble list of values. Then they put it aside, never looking at it again. And you wonder why employees turn bitter and cynical?

Common Values

Values can be a single word (like *discipline*), or they can be a phrase or sentence (like *We always meet our goals*). That gives you great flexibility. You can take words that appear in this list and use them by themselves or weave them into sentences that have meaning for you and your group. Use this list to spark your thinking.

accountability
achievement
aggressive
always hit our
    numbers
always meet
    deadlines
continuous
    improvement
continuous
    learning
contrarian
cooperation
courage
courtesy
creativity
crisp
curiosity
customer focus
dignity
direct
discipline
dissent
diversity
elegance
empowerment
encourage
fairness

financial strength
fun
goal-oriented
hard work
honesty
honor
imagination
independence
innovation
integrity
justice
keep promises
leadership
lean and mean
learning organiza-
    tion
loyalty
merit
never compromise
no excuses
no politics
on time
operational
    excellence
originality
participation
performance
perseverance

persistence
pride
product excel-
    lence
professionalism
punctuality
quality
reliability
reputation
respect
responsibility
safety
service to others
service excellence
speed
standardize
steady
systematize
teamwork
team players
technical excel-
    lence
technological
    proficiency
timeliness
trust
we deliver
welcome change

Values must be lived. Chosen well, they won't wear out from overuse. They'll become more durable with time.

Measure your efforts, and those of your people, by values. Promote those who operate in line with them. Reprimand or fire those who don't. Keep values in mind whenever you make a decision. Remind people often of the values and why they are important. Let them know, in every way you can, that the values are real and must be acknowledged in every organizational practice or policy.

The Agile Manager's Checklist

✔ Stand on a foundation of values.

✔ Use values to shape your organization or department and the direction it's headed.

✔ Remember: Values outlive goals. Choose them well.

✔ Live the values. Too many organizations come up with a fine list of values, then ignore them.

✔ Measure people and business efforts by your values.

Chapter Three

Follow Up with a Mission (And Maybe a Vision)

The Agile Manager stared up at the corner of his office, a pen-cil between his teeth. Along with values, he needed to come up with a mission statement. "For whom?" He'd asked his boss. "For the company, the division, this department, me?"

"I don't know," said his boss. "Don't worry about it—you won't be graded. If it's real important, and they want something else, they'll shoot it back."

Let's pretend I really care about this, thought the Agile Manager. "And maybe you should," piped up one of the less-cynical voices in his head. "A good mission can galvanize people and give them a cause to work for. You'll get more out of them. Why else would non-owners work hundred-hour weeks as they do at high-tech start-ups?"

Good point, internal critic of mine. OK: What we do here in a way defines the division, and a big chunk of the company. I can do a mission statement that covers all of us at once.

The Agile Manager, who headed product development for the medical-instruments division of a large, diversified company, thought of the possibilities.

Whom do we exist for? Shareholders? Nah. We serve society. We serve hospitals and doctors. We serve purchasing agents.

That's it: "To provide purchasing agents with wonderful products they can get congratulated on for buying." Ha.

He wrote, "To aid physicians in diagnosing life-threatening diseases." Then, "To help physicians heal patients." Not quite.

"Hey Steve," he yelled out to his assistant after a few minutes. "What do you think of this for the mission statement: 'To help physicians and medical personnel diagnose diseases and patient problems ever faster using the most innovative technology.'?"

"Try again," came the retort. That figures, thought the Agile Manager. If I could do this exercise in three minutes, how valuable could it be? I better talk to Anna, Mark, Andy, Rolf, Wanda, and a few others. I need input, and a little history. Also, maybe it would be fun to create a goal that embodied the new values and mission. Maybe something about cutting development time . . ."

Leaders need a strong point of view regarding:

- What purpose the company or department serves;
- Where it's going and why;
- What its ultimate potential is;
- What defines the work it does;
- What defines results.

These are all large questions. One way to boil them down is to answer them by way of mission statement, and possibly a vision statement. A well-crafted mission or vision statement gives people a purpose, beyond a paycheck, for working; it acts as a guideline for forming strategies and goals, and for making decisions; and it focuses efforts.

Let's Define Terms

The words *vision* and *mission* have been thrown around so much by consultants, writers, and corporate staffers that they are often used interchangeably.

Since Moses didn't come down from the mountain with definitions for these words chiseled in stone, I'll define them as follows:

A **mission** defines your organization's reason for being. It embodies the contribution you make to society and the purpose you serve. It serves as a guide to all employees, including managers, by defining explicitly the work of the company or the department.

A *vision* is a large, overarching, grand goal, presented in clear, simple, concrete, easily visualized terms. A good vision gives people a cause to work for (as can a mission).

MISSION

Creating a moving mission statement is absolutely essential to good leadership. And crafting a good one is well within the reach of anybody.

What I call mission, Peter Drucker calls "the idea of the business." In his words, it "defines a satisfaction to be supplied to the market or a knowledge to be made effective in economic performance." Drucker says that by its nature, a mission "establishes objectives, it sets goals and direction. It determines what results are meaningful and what measurements truly appropriate."

Best Tip

Create a moving mission statement for your group. It's essential to good leadership (and profitability!).

While Drucker here is referring to the company as a whole, his definition works well at a division or departmental level as well. At the department level, for instance, "market" can refer to customers inside or outside the company.

A good mission packs a wallop. Let's look at some examples:

Girls Scouts of America: "The purpose of Girl Scouting is to inspire girls with the highest ideals of character, conduct, patriotism, and service that they may become happy and resourceful citizens." This one couldn't be more pointed or virtuous. It defines the work to be done and gives employees and volunteers a cause to subscribe to.

Coca-Cola Company: "We exist to create value for our share owners on a long-term basis by building a business that enhances the Coca-Cola Company's trademarks. This also is our ultimate commitment."

This is not a mission that excites anyone but senior managers and shareholders, but one that is simple, focused, and guiding. Fortunately, it continues in a more inspiring vein: "As the world's largest beverage company, we refresh that world. We do this by developing superior soft drinks . . ." Wow! That's visionary.

Harvard's John F. Kennedy School of Government: "[To serve] the public interest by preparing leaders for service in government and other institutions in democratic societies, and by contributing to the solution of important public problems." That noble mission undoubtedly adds energy to the institution and its people (and perhaps makes students and faculty a tad arrogant).

Make sure your mission statement concentrates and directs effort.

Fast Company **(a business magazine):** "*Fast Company* aims to be the handbook of the business revolution. We will chronicle the changes under way in how companies create and compete, highlight the new practices shaping how work gets done, showcase teams who are inventing the future and reinventing business. Most of all, we will equip the people exploring this uncharted territory with the tools, techniques, models, and mindsets they need."

I'm sure this stirs the souls of those who work for the company—they're inciting and participating in a revolution!—and it does an excellent job defining what is, and hence what is not, its business.

FedEx: "To deliver packages intact and on time." This says it all. And it makes measuring the success of the mission easy—if it's not intact or on-time, FedEx fails.

Johnson & Johnson: "To alleviate pain and suffering." (In the words of founder R. W. Johnson.) Compare this ennobling corporate mission with the first part of Coke's.

A good mission statement concentrates and directs effort. *Fast Company* knows, for example, that it shouldn't do articles on sailboat racing, or spin off a magazine on issues of interest to chief financial officers. Coke's mission makes it clear that protecting its trademarks is of vital importance, and that it had better be careful, therefore, about how it licenses its logo.

Create an Organizational Mission

There is no formula for creating a mission statement. That's good. If there were, the mission of every organization would sound the same. Besides, too much depends on the nature of your company, the industry, and the character of your management team.

What follows, then, are guidelines only.

Where to start. The main thing in creating a mission is to identify the customers you serve and the value you bring to them. In addition, the mission should focus people and guide their decisions.

Best Tip
Circulate drafts of the mission to get feedback. This is especially important if you want buy-in from your people.

What do you do well? What do you excel at? How do you add value to those you serve? If you're in an established business or department, your mission should be fairly easy to identify. After all, if you weren't satisfying the marketplace, you wouldn't have made it past the start-up phase.

Provide a higher purpose. Ideally, your mission statement provides a lofty goal. Only that produces extraordinary performance from employees. I don't know whether Internet software firm Netscape has an explicit mission or not, but an implied mission, and one doing a wonderful job motivating employees, is "To beat Microsoft."

A mission is not a financial goal. I recently saw a "mission" that said, "Our mission is to achieve sales of $1 billion by 2001."

This is a fine goal, but a mission? Whom will it motivate besides shareholders or those few in a position to profit by such growth? How does it define the work to be done? What direction does it give? What does it say about a contribution to a specific market? **Get the words right.** The hard part in crafting a mission is getting the words just right. Having a lengthy mission isn't necessarily a sin, but short, clear, and sharp is more motivating. Use clear, concrete language that anyone can grasp immediately. For example, rather than say something like "Our mission is to excel in the global field of agricultural genetic engineering," say "Our mission is to improve the productivity of farmers worldwide through the genetic engineering of field crops."

Unless you're the owner of a company you founded with a specific mission in mind, write a draft and circulate it among your peers. You'll get good feedback. And people may have a different, illuminating take on the work your company or department does. Further, those you include will help you spread the word once you finish the job. You'll gain immediate buy-in from influential people.

Create a Departmental Mission

Managers can gain all the motivational and economic benefits discussed thus far by creating a mission for their departments. Missions are especially important for the morale of those working in support services. They rarely get the glory heaped on line workers or those involved in new-product efforts.

If you're in information technology, for example, your mission might be "To provide a powerful communications network that helps the company satisfy customers and beat rivals." Or, "To maintain the network and provide solutions for hardware and software problems in the minimum amount of time."

If you're in human resources: "To find the highest-caliber candidates for key jobs within the company." Or, "To provide training that brings our workforce up to and beyond world-class standards."

If you're in R&D: "To provide the company with innovative technologies and product ideas that surpass any offered by competing companies."

If you're in maintenance: "To keep all systems running efficiently so employees can achieve the company's goals."

Short-term Missions

The kind of missions we've been discussing are high-level, overarching reasons for being. They are essential for conducting business energetically and efficiently.

You need a mission for short-term projects, too. Every team, task force, or committee should have a mission.

These needn't be elaborate. If you're on a new-product team, for instance, your mission could be as simple (and as challenging) as "Get the product out the door by January 15." Or if you're on a committee investigating industrywide benefits practices, it could be "Have recommendations ready by the next Executive Committee meeting."

Missions Can Change

A good mission will last you a while, and maybe forever. But don't be afraid to change it. I'm sure Coke's founder didn't give two thoughts about exploiting its trademarks—he wanted to get Coke inside as many humans as he could.

VISION

A vision, recall, is a large, grand goal, and it's presented in clear, simple, concrete, easily visualized terms. Based on that definition, only a few of the things most organizations call vision statements qualify.

Further, many of the best visions are never written down and promoted as the "company vision statement," yet they are well-known by those in the company.

Here are some examples of what I term visions:

Henry Ford: "A car for every family." Until Ford came along, automobiles were considered strictly for the wealthy.

Bill Gates and Paul Allen: "A computer on every desktop." This is an interesting example, because Gates and Allen weren't in the hardware business. But they knew—earlier than just about anyone—that the key to making this vision a reality was software so useful that everyone would want a computer.

Daimler-Chrysler: "We will be the premier North American Car and Truck Company." (Chrysler calls this a mission.)

Motorola's Lexicus Division: "[T]o be the world's leading supplier of handwriting and speech recognition technologies which enable the input and retrieval of information without a keyboard."

Don't bother with a vision unless you own the company or are leading a change effort.

Note that Lexicus is envisioning a huge market now barely in its infancy, together with its place in it.

Steve Jobs (while at Apple): "To make insanely great computers." Pundits like to disparage this vision—because it neglects the real needs of the marketplace—but I bet it was pretty motivating for Apple's employees.

Al Dunlap (while head of Scott Paper): "To become a company on par with industry leaders like Kimberly-Clark and to become a household name throughout the world."

As you can see, visions, even good ones, are a mixed bag of ideas. Some are company-focused, some are market-focused. Some have a "change the world" component; others don't.

The common characteristic is that the person or company envisions a reality far beyond where it is presently, a reality a company can take part in, if not create. A good vision makes your spine tingle.

The Trouble with Most Visions

Most visions are too long and read like a list of platitudes written by a consultant. (Most probably are.) Few are unique.

A prominent chemical company's lengthy vision, for instance, includes this:

"[Our company] is a profitable, professional, responsible, growth-oriented, customer-driven team that supplies high-quality products and services while maintaining sensitivity to our employees and the community."

I'd call this more a collection of values than a vision. And I'd call it that only if people actually worked in harmony with them and were measured by them.

And what distinguishes it? It could be the vision statement of any one of hundreds of companies.

Create a Vision—Maybe

It's hard to come up with a really good vision. It's also not necessary, I don't believe, in most cases. A good mission suffices.

Also, a vision has to come from the top. Unless it does, it is utterly meaningless. No one below the CEO and her top lieutenants can set the company on a course to change the world. And it's doubtful a department head could come up with and pursue a worthwhile vision without extraordinary autonomy and resources.

Two exceptions: First, when you're trying to change people's behavior, even at the departmental level, you should have a vision of what you want the company or department to become. We'll cover that aspect of visioning in chapter ten, on leading change. Second, a start-up should have a vision. It'll help people survive the lean days with good humor.

Vision-creating Questions

These questions will get you thinking grandly, which is where you want your mind to be when thinking about a vision:

- In what ways would society suffer without us?
- What is the extent of our potential reach?
- What satisfaction can we deliver that will have, potentially, a huge impact on people?

- Can we create a market with our product?
- How can we change the world, given hard work and good ideas?
- What unexploited potential exists in the company?
- How big can we grow?
- What does our gut tell us about our role in the industry?

These questions don't require rigorous analysis. They are a starting point that should enable you to come up with a sentence or two (at the most) that describes the world you want to be in—or, better, create—some years hence.

Best Tip

In creating a vision, forget about logic. Visions are about grand dreams, not common sense.

People often counsel vision makers to create a vision that seems within reach. That makes logical sense, but a vision isn't about logic. It's about dreams and aspirations. What if Gates and Allen had amended their dream to something that, at the time, would have made much more sense: "A computer on every tenth desk"?

People want to make a difference. They want to be in on something big. They want to work for an important purpose. Give it to them, and they'll commit their lives to you.

Remember: If it makes your spine tingle, you've got a good vision. If not, go back to the drawing board.

Here's a few examples, made up out of whole cloth:

Pharmaceutical company: "Rid the world of AIDS."

Software company: "To make every accountant a financial genius."

Grain company: "To triple the yield of every farm field."

Furniture maker: "To get our furniture in every showroom in North America."

Aerospace company: "To help colonize Mars."

A good vision enlarges the thinking of employees and helps them think "out of the box" to come up with radical improvements. If you're going to get to Mars one day, you won't worry about shaving five hours off the trip to the moon. You'll discover how to get there in a few minutes—then on to Mars.

Make It Unique

I once heard management guru Gary Hamel tell an interesting story. He was addressing a group of a large company's most senior executives. He said something like, "Now I'd like to read to you the vision statement of your top competitor." He read it, and the managers drank it in, nodding thoughtfully.

Hamel continued with his talk for a few minutes. Then he stopped and said, "I want to tell you something. That vision statement I just read was *yours*—and not a single one of you recognized it. So do you think it has any meaning or value whatsoever for your employees?"

If your vision isn't unique, and if it doesn't stir your people, don't embarrass anyone by making it public.

The Agile Manager's Checklist

✔ Create a mission statement. It focuses your people and guides their decisions.

✔ In your mission, give people a lofty goal or role to live up to.

✔ If you need to, change your mission.

✔ Think twice before you hire a consultant to craft a mission or vision statement.

SECTION II

Mission into Action

*"Leadership is the ability to decide what is to be
done, and then to get others to do it."*

Dwight D. Eisenhower

Chapter Four

Set Strategies, Goals, And Standards

"Tony," said the Agile Manager. "Speed is one of our values. We live by it. We always have. The founders instilled that value from the beginning, and they talked or wrote about it all the time."

"Yeah, but . . ."

"No 'yeah buts.' It now takes us an average of six months to go from conception to prototype. That's ridiculous. While we're fiddling with designs, Murphy Technology is past prototype and into production. If we don't get faster, they'll bury us."

"Yeah, but we have better designs—"

"No 'yeah buts'! I don't care if every product of ours wins an award. They get stuff into the marketplace faster. The customers I talk to say sure, they love our quality. But they love the innovative products Murphy passes in front of their noses on a monthly basis. Murphy, to hospitals, is excitement. And that translates into sales. Besides, they are fast at fixing flaws, too. So why not toss products on the market and see what flies?"

Tony said nothing for a moment. "Well, what do you want?"

"Two months."

"Two months!? Are you joking? Hassan and Evans in fabrication take two months to wipe their noses. Impossible."

"It is possible, and we're going to do it. If it makes you feel any better, I'm paying Hassan and Evans a visit right after this. In fact, I'm paying everybody a visit. Now, we're going to meet Friday at 10:00. We'll talk about how to turn this value, speed, into reality in product development. See you there." The Agile Manager waltzed out the door.

Tony stared at the product design on his computer screen. Two months, he thought. It can't happen—but it would be great if it could. We could start pumping out products like crazy. And he's right—we satisfy people, but we don't excite them. It'd be fun to do that once in a while . . .

Among the gravest mistakes organizations make is to go through the trouble of coming up with values and mission, then forget to tie these things to strategies, goals and standards, and operational business practices.

To say "forget" is putting it kindly. Many managers have no intention of translating a vision and values into reality. That's the messy part. It's hard work.

But good leaders make sure it gets done.

Strategies Make the Mission Sing

"Strategies," says Stephen Covey, "tie your vision and values to customers."

For example, the vision of Microsoft's Gates and Allen, to see a computer on every desktop, suggested a strategy early on: To set the standards and create the software by which people would operate computers.

A clear mission or vision doesn't guarantee workable strategies, but it makes your job easier. A good mission, remember, keeps you from getting into things that don't or shouldn't concern you. It keeps you channeled into productive areas you know well.

Strategy is a large subject, but here's a simple set of questions for creating one. Keeping your mission or vision in mind, ask these questions to come up with strategies and goals:

- What is our advantage or unique selling proposition?
- Who or what is our market?
- How can we reach it?
- What do we need in the way of people, money, or other resources to fulfill our mission?
- Who is going to do each job?
- What deadlines do we need?
- What measures will tell us we've reached the goal?

Say your vision is to get your line of furniture into every showroom in North America. If you're presently represented in only three states, you could probably break that mission down into regions, like New England, Southeast, and Mid-Atlantic.

Who is the market? The 225 upscale furniture stores in New England.

How will we reach them? A combination of in-house sales reps and independent reps, furniture shows, and direct marketing.

Best Tip

Tie your mission and values to your strategy and everyday goals and business practices.

What are our advantages? Award-winning designs for a contemporary lifestyle, and an industry-leading just-in-time delivery system.

What kind of our resources will we need? We'll need a marketing budget of $1.2 million a year, four in-house reps, and three independent reps.

Who is going to do each job? Phil will handle Massachusetts and Rhode Island, John will handle Connecticut, and Betsy will handle Maine, Vermont and New Hampshire.

What are the deadlines? Twenty-five percent penetration into stores in six months, 50 percent in a year, 100 percent in two years.

How will we know we've reached the goal? We'll count, store by store, until we are at 90 percent penetration or better, then we'll staff up and hit the Mid-Atlantic region.

This is greatly simplified. Coming up with precise figures like these takes weeks of study and analysis. (And months or years to install a competition-beater like just-in-time inventory replenishment.) Plus, you'll succeed or fail on the strength of your products and other advantages; the tactics you employ to get goods into stores; the administrative policies that make it easy, or hard, to do business with you; and competitor strategies.

Turn Values into Goals and Standards

Your values will also help you set explicit standards and goals.

Some values lend themselves to easy definition and measurement. A good example is "speed." Companies have made real improvements in results by cutting cycle times, order-fulfillment time, and machine-changeover times.

It's not difficult to measure how long your operations or processes take to complete, then set goals to speed them up.

But first it takes the will to say: "It now takes us seventy-two hours to fill an order. By the end of the year, I want that figure down to twenty-four hours." Also, because you can't order such a change, no matter what your position on the organization chart, it takes teamwork, good human-relations skills, and communications skills.

Don't be scared off by values that seem to resist quantification or measurement. Say a key value of yours is excellent customer service. You can still set standards, such as these:

- Answer the phone in two rings;
- Process applications in twenty-four hours;
- Have customer information accessible from every work station;
- Always solve a customer problem within a day;
- Ship orders in one day;
- Don't hesitate to offer a refund to angry customers.

Another example: Most companies profess to be "innovative." What, exactly, does that mean? How do you define and measure it? By new products or new patents? Good ideas put to use?

Process innovations? How you define it is up to you, but define it you must if you want that value to motivate people.

Ditch Useless Values

If you can't take each of your stated values and turn it into a meaningful, concrete goal or standard, get rid of it. Otherwise it will stand for nothing.

Set ambitious goals for your group or department. Doing so will unleash energy and creativity.

In trying to translate "courtesy" into a concrete set of standards, for example, you may decide that the word "courtesy" is not precisely what you want. You really want "service," which you find easier to define and make explicit for employees.

Turning values into concrete goals and standards keeps you honest. It ensures that your values statement is something more than a laundry list of platitudes that can't be acted upon.

Set Ambitious Goals

Good leaders set goals that cause people to stretch. Incremental improvements are fine and should be encouraged, but it's the ambitious goals that stir the blood and let loose innovation.

It's said that Boeing Corporation often sets "bet the farm" goals for itself by throwing all its resources and expertise into the current project, like the recent 777 or, years ago, the 727. The goal is to succeed—or die trying. Such goals are probably necessary, given Boeing's vision: "People working together as one global company for aerospace leadership."

Setting such goals unleashes the energy and creativity of the workforce—and it can keep you far ahead of rivals.

Goals can be ambitious even at the departmental level. In many spheres of business, faster turnover is better. Turning over work in your department faster makes you more productive and valuable. So give people ambitious goals for speeding up trans-actions, projects, or assets you oversee.

Spellbinding Goals and Standards

Good leaders know that there is some magic involved in reach-ing ambitious goals or gaining companywide compliance with values. Leaders add, therefore, a bit of drama to the goal to cap-ture the imagination.

Sometimes a performance is called for. The late Sam Walton, for example, was a brilliant performer, as well as strategist. He frequently led employees in the Wal-Mart cheer, and he spent the last years of his life exhorting employees to do their part in helping the company reach $125 billion in sales.

Spellbinders can also be a word or slogan that becomes in-house shorthand for a particular goal. For example: Motorola's "Six Sigma." It's a quality goal that means, roughly, two defects per billion. Repeated often enough, such a phrase becomes an incantation.

Dress up values so people can understand and put them to use. Here are two examples from Wal-Mart, which is without peer in instilling values in the culture.

1. The Sundown Rule. Employees complete jobs, like re-quests from customers or fellow workers, the same day (before sundown). According to Wal-Mart, this rule supports three val-ues: respect for the individual, customer service, and a striving for excellence.

2. The Ten-foot Attitude. This is another rule to put the concept of customer service into action. It means that whenever you come within ten feet of customers, you look them in the eye, say hello, and ask if they need help.

Met Your Goal? Set the Next One

Having a potent mission and a good foundation of values ensure you never run out of goals. You've reached six sigma? Your value of dedication to quality means you can get on with the next. How about going for seven sigma. You've cut product-development time in half? Cut it in half again. Your goods are in every furniture store in the country? Get 'em into European and Asian stores. Or double your sales with your existing base. The best-run companies never let goals or standards get stale. If yours don't motivate, replace them. And if the underlying mission and values get shopworn, replace those, too.

Mission, Values, and Goals Create Unity

The best companies operate as a team in the best sense of the word: They are all playing by the same rules, eyes focused on the same goal. The goal is bigger than any of their individual concerns, so they willingly help each other in service of the mission. Backbiting, negative politics, and sniping is rare.

You can *feel* good leadership at a company. People are friendly and energetic. They talk about their work and the work of the company in glowing terms because they give life meaning.

None of this means that the company or department is a happy family. It's more like a sports team on top of the league standings. Not everybody likes each other, not everybody approves of what gets done, and people sometimes argue about how to succeed. But they all have their eyes on the ultimate goal—winning.

The Agile Manager's Checklist

✔ Tie mission to strategy and goals. It's hard, messy work, but worth it.

✔ Use your values to set operational standards and goals.

✔ If you can't turn a value into a quantifiable goal or standard, then drop it.

✔ Once you've reached a goal, don't rest. Set another one.

Chapter Five

You're a Role Model

"So let me get this straight," said the Agile Manager. "I write up a purchase order for housings I don't need. You process the order up to the point of shipment. Then, after the first of next month, I cancel the order."

"Right," said Schmidt, the sales manager for a company that both supplied and bought from the Agile Manager's company.

"And you get points toward your contest because you get the order just before it ends. You'll go to Hawaii."

"Right," said Schmidt, snickering. "I need to get a few more points to get ahead of some jerk in our Omaha office. And it's safe, because I'm the sales manager. Who's gonna question me?" He laughed again.

"Oops," said the Agile Manager. "Someone just walked in. I'll call you back." Slimebucket, he thought as he hung up.

"Steve!" he called through the closed office door.

"Yeah, boss?" said Steve cheerfully as he walked in.

"Listen to this." He told his assistant the story.

"Hmm," said Steve, wondering how his boss would handle it.

"Now his best friend at his company is Walker," said the Agile Manager, "who buys from us all the time. Schmidt knows that. The implication is that if I don't go along with this, Walker will stop

buying from us or at least cut back. And Walker is as bad as
Schmidt. Sales people here say you'd better buy him a real nice
lunch if you want a decent order. Schmidt is also friends with Jill
Menendez in our purchasing department. His wife went to school
with her."
   "What are you going to do?" asked Steve.
   "Good question. I'll let you know." Steve left and the Agile
Manager propped his feet on the desk. Within ten seconds he
swung them back on the floor and stood up. You either have stan-
dards or you don't, he thought. He opened his door, then went
back and dialed up Schmidt.
   "Schmitty? I can't do it. Sorry."
   "Oh come on—what's the big deal? Your people do this kind of
thing all the time. I was just talking to Bob Walker about it yester-
day. That's where I got the idea."
   Liar, thought the Agile Manager. "I'm sorry."
   "I'm sure you are," Schmidt sputtered as he hung up.

Your published values, mission, or vision aren't worth a dime
unless you live them, without exception.

A friend of mine once told me a revealing story. He worked
with a company that made a big deal out of honesty in dealing
with customers and vendors.

He was having drinks and talking shop with a few people in
the department, including his boss. They got the bill and the
boss paid it. As they left, the boss said gleefully, "She forgot the
last round of drinks and the hors d'ouevres! We saved at least
twenty bucks!"

My friend didn't think much about it until a year later. He
was having a dinner meeting with his new boss and a few others. The bill came, and the boss looked it over. He called over
the waiter and said, "I think you forgot to include the second
bottle of wine." It was expensive; the waiter was most grateful.

While the first incident didn't make much of an impression
on my friend—he didn't much care for that boss anyway—the
second made a deep and lasting one.

It Takes Time—and Consistency

Now my friend wouldn't have walked through a burning house to save his new boss just after the dinner incident. But over time his admiration and respect grew to such a point that he would have followed him anywhere. His values gave him substance and power. And you always knew where he stood on an issue.

Tom Melohn took over North American Tool and Die and turned it into a prime supplier for companies like Hewlett-Packard and NUMMI, the Toyota-GM joint venture. When he took over, however, morale and profitability were at low points.

Melohn had a vision of a new and different workplace, one in which trust permeated the environment. He wanted people to trust him, he wanted to trust them to do a good job, and he wanted customers to trust the company to satisfy their requirements. That trust, writes Melohn in *The New Partnership*, took about two years to build. He built it on daily acts that, over time, recreated the work environment.

Melohn showed his employees he trusted them, for example, by letting shop-floor workers guide visiting VIPs and potential customers on plant tours. Melohn would introduce the worker to the guest, then walk away. That sent a powerful message.

Tom Melohn and my friend's boss both showed something absolutely critical to good leadership: consistency. People will believe you only when you act in accordance with your stated beliefs—always. If you're honest sometimes and not others, you are not honest. If you talk about quality and demand it except when you're struggling to meet an end-of-the-month quota, you don't believe in quality. And everyone knows it.

Get in the Thick of It

Leaders must be seen to be heard. Tom Peters suggests you spend at least 50 percent of your time on top priority items—in full view of your people.

Some leaders do better than that. Ray Kroc of McDonald's spent countless hours in the chain's restaurants. If he arrived during a rush time, he'd get out a broom and sweep the floor, bus tables, or pick up litter in the parking lot. Staff loved seeing the boss living his ideals. It sent a message that McDonald's policies apply to everyone, and that the crew—including Kroc if he were there—were all in it together.

"Ace" Greenberg, chairman of investment bank Bear, Stearns, sits on the trading floor in the midst of the chaos. He likes to be, he says, where the electricity is. He also notes that his station allows him to solve problems on the spot.

Best Tip

Live the values you espouse. For the most part, people are watching you, not listening to you.

He undoubtedly serves as a potent symbol of the firm's values for the employees surrounding him.

Get out and talk to people. Be approachable. Take their input and feedback. Each encounter helps build the blocks that create a strong organization.

Rank Should Not Mean Privilege

As Peter Drucker has said, "Rank is not privilege. It's responsibility."

Executives sometimes do dumb things. They give a speech to employees about frugality, then jump into a limo and zip off to a trendy restaurant for lunch. Or they prattle on about teamwork and how everyone is a leader. Then they make sure that no other "leader" gets the parking spot closest to the door. Or they talk incessantly about "participatory management" yet never get around to actually inviting participation.

If you are not living the values you advocate, everyone knows it. And the lowest-level employees are among the smartest in doing one thing—watching what you do rather than listening to what you say.

Cleaning and maintenance company ServiceMaster keeps its managers humble by requiring them to do the jobs their people do a few days a year. They clean toilets, change light bulbs, or kill cockroaches. Doing so reminds managers exactly who does the work that pays bills. It also shows them the job from the worker's perspective, including its frustrations, challenges, and rewards. That makes them more sensitive when issuing orders or planning policy.

Be Decisive—at Times

When it comes to acting in accordance with your mission and values, act or decide quickly. Again, your people are watching.

Don't waver, for instance, when faced with a decision that requires you to act in line with values. Say, for example, the "customer is always right" in your area. One day, you get a call from a customer who would like to return a large order. What do you say? "Yes, of course," no matter how painful the decision is to make.

Best Tip

Call or visit a customer every day or every week. You'll send a strong message about what's important.

There are times to be indecisive. Once in a while, it's important to bite your tongue. If, for example, you value independent thinking, and you're trying to get a person or team to make more decisions, help out by keeping your silence.

Good leaders are also indecisive when it comes to the daily practice of a job or task. They defer to those closest to the work, who know the job better.

Stay Close to Customers

Good leaders focus on customers. You set an example to others by maintaining contact with them.

There are organizational ways to do that. A German manufacturer of farm machinery owns a retail store in each of its major markets. Managers take turns staffing the stores so they can get direct feedback from the end users of their products.

I once helped produce a monthly publication read by tens of thousands in more than a hundred countries. Yet I rarely talked to customers. So I devised ways to encourage subscribers to call me, mainly by touting my expertise in referring them to problem-solving sources. I also encouraged customer service people to transfer calls from dissatisfied customers to me, and I answered the phones during weekly staff meetings.

I learned a lot in these sessions, and they also had symbolic value. People saw me acting in accordance with one of my core values: staying close to the customer.

Do Real Work

It used to be said that a manager shouldn't actually do anything but manage. If that were ever true, it sure isn't now.

A friend of mine worked for a company in which the owner did nothing except collect a weekly paycheck. He'd delegated everything. Yet he still wanted to be first in line to take all the praise for the success of the firm.

The practical result: Everyone held him in contempt, considering him a phony. Good people bailed out, and the company muddled along, performing far below its potential.

Do real work. That's work that contributes directly to the products or services that you sell to customers. Executives in publishing houses, even CEOs, still acquire and edit a few titles a year. They want to keep the skills that got them there polished, but they also want to show those in positions below them that they are helping turn the wheel.

Best Tip

Do real work alongside your people. They'll respect you more if you're in the trenches next to them.

Overcome Setbacks and Get Things Done

Sometimes you face threats to your values or mission. Imagine you head a department, and one of your key values is "We always make our sales quota." Time is running out, and your quota looks harder to reach by the hour.

Take the initiative, but not by having all the answers and ordering employee A to do this and employee B to do that.

Round up the troops, tell them the problem, and ask for help solving it. Together you'll think of better solutions.

In the case just mentioned, someone may remember that a certain high-volume account hasn't been called on this month. Someone else may remember that there have been lots of unfilled orders due to a shortage of a certain product. Maybe the problem doesn't really exist.

Whatever you do, roll up your sleeves, live up to your values, and meet your goals. If you say, "Oh well, maybe we can make it up next month," or "Maybe we can backdate next month's orders to meet this month's quota," you're sending a message loud and clear: "Don't worry about our mission, values, and goals. We can sidestep them."

> **Best Tip**
>
> In decision making, encourage dissent. If there is none, appoint a devil's advocate. Different points of view are a necessary ingredient in making sound decisions.

Encourage Dissent

A politician in supposedly democratic South Korea said, in a recent radio report, "We must suppress this group and put its leaders in prison. Its ideas could infect the rest of the people and then we would have a crisis."

This politician was only doing what comes naturally to sham leaders standing on shaky beliefs or values. He did not believe in the strength of his own values and ideas, nor those that built his country.

If your values and mission are sound, you can invite dissent without fear. Paul Galvin of Motorola insisted on dissent. He thought it essential to making good decisions.

Tolerate Mistakes

Strong leaders also put up with mistakes. Not stupid mistakes, or mistakes made twice, but well-meaning, intelligent mistakes made in line with the company's values and mission.

Tolerating mistakes is essential if one of your stated values is about the importance of taking risks.

Any failure contains many lessons—like how not to do something, or where your view of the market is flawed. That's why Johnson & Johnson's Robert Wood Johnson once said, "Failure is our most important product."

If people are to put their skills, imagination, creativity, and will to work for you, they must have your confidence. In tolerating mistakes, you are showing confidence in them and their abilities.

Deal with the Lazy, Malcontents, and Evildoers

All your efforts at boosting values and showing dedication to a noble mission are for naught if you permit substandard performers, or those who mock your values or the mission, to remain on the payroll. Doing so is one of the quickest morale killers known to humanity. Prune such people carefully and legally, but don't let them linger. One poor worker can poison the group.

The Agile Manager's Checklist

✔ Be consistent in living and applying your values.
✔ If necessary, do the dirty work—and let your people see you doing it.
✔ Remember: Rank is responsibility more than privilege.
✔ Put up with mistakes. It's part of the learning process.
✔ Don't let malcontents linger. They'll poison the staff.

Chapter Six

Communicate with Skill

The Agile Manager stopped Anita in the hallway. "How are you doing with those design specs?" he asked.

"They are about done," she answered brightly. "And we'll finish them in record time. It sure helps to meet with the manufacturing people regularly. And I wish all meetings were as good as those are—we have an agenda, we move through it bang, bang, bang, and we're out of there. All we talk about is, 'Will this work? Will that work?' and we get answers."

"Not like the old days, I can tell you," said the Agile Manager, chuckling. "When I first started, the plant manager wouldn't talk to anyone in product development. I once wanted some information about a product delivery, and he glared at me and said, 'I report to the CEO, not you,' and walked away."

The Agile Manager continued, "Great to hear that things are smoother. We've got the conception-to-prototype average down to four months, which means we've got two months to go. What do you need to get your work done faster?"

"Oh, I don't know. The usual. More money, more clout, more people," said Anita.

"You can't have more money or people, at least not now. More *bodies sometimes slows things down, anyway. What else?"*

"I suppose we could have more cooperation from Jim in R&D. He acts like he's doing research that will get him the Nobel Prize one day. Makes him hard to deal with. Also, he doesn't have what I would call a 'product focus.'"

"I'm becoming a pest in R&D, because it's one of the biggest bottlenecks in cutting development time. I didn't know Jim was one of the problems, though. Thanks. I'll nose around some more— without implicating you," said the Agile Manager.

"You know, he continued, "we'll go down in history if we get down to 120 days." He then flashed a warm smile and raised his voice slightly as he said, "Thanks a lot for your help. You're doing a great job. Keep it up."

Leaders not only live their mission, values, and goals, but they do their best to ensure everyone else does. That requires good communication skills and the desire to talk incessantly about concerns.

Broadcast Your Agenda

One way or another, talk about your mission, values, and goals with whomever you meet. Put them in memos, on your intranet Web site or personal home page, with your signature at the end of e-mail messages, on the bulletin board, and anywhere else you think they might do some good.

Surround people with messages regarding your agenda. After a while, they'll tune out such messages consciously, but you'll still hit them at an unconscious level.

And don't let your noble mission go to waste. If you've done a good job with it, the mission gives people an opportunity to be part of something grand. It makes them feel important.

Acknowledge Resistance

Don't pretend everyone backs your agenda strongly. Some will do so unquestioningly, some will do so based on the logic of your arguments or the force of your emotions, and some will have to be won over slowly. Then there's that small minority that sits harping in the corner no matter what.

In meetings, or in a memo, answer the cynics and defeatists. There's no need to name names.

Disarm your critics before they pounce on you. Do that by anticipating and overcoming their objections.

Just say, "I know some people think it's impossible to reduce our collection period from forty-two days to twenty-five days. I'm here to say it is possible. We can do it, but I need the help of all of you. We're already down to thirty-six days, and here's how we'll chop off another six. First we . . ."

People like to give leaders the benefit of the doubt. And few like chronic naysayers. Disarming the critics will win you a few converts and solidify your position among others, at the very least. Peer pressure may then sway the doom-and-gloom crowd.

Use Imagery and Symbols

A good symbol or logo can focus attention on changes or express values in concentrated form. My local bank, for example, changed its corporate structure and began to focus on dealing with customers by linking with them electronically. At the heart of its new logo, appearing on all signs and bank communications, is the lynx.

I'm not sure what it means to the bank (except for a play on words—lynx/links), but to me the lynx stands for speed and agility. These are qualities I like.

Rosenbluth International adopted the salmon as its in-house mascot. Why? The salmon swims upstream. It bucks trends. It takes a contrary approach to solving problems. Also, it no doubt signals to employees that they're not like all the other fish that swim in the sea. They're special.

Show Enthusiasm

No one is going to care about what *you* care about unless you're enthusiastic about it. And if you hope to accomplish an extraordinary goal or vision, you'd better be downright passionate.

As a salesman, I've seen how a little passion and enthusiasm can turn bored, indifferent store owners and buyers into believers in a product. And all in a minute or two.

I used that same enthusiasm to train others to sell. Enthusiasm for a goal moves people, I discovered, because most don't have compelling goals of their own. They are happy to be handed a few goals they can believe in and make them feel important.

Persevere

A good friend of mine manages a group of customer-service representatives. They'd seen other managers come and go, and they had learned to lay low during the honeymoon phase. Whatever new initiatives came up, they knew, were likely to die.

My friend, however, wanted to help the company grow. She knew that these people, with more customer contact than anyone, could bring in new revenue.

She introduced a program to increase sales per customer. The program was nothing manipulative or browbeating—it just reminded customers how useful product A or B might be in their

Best Tip

Develop passion and enthusiasm for what you're doing. It moves people better than well-constructed arguments.

lives, or how they could take advantage of a special one-day-only discount on product C.

She sweetened these programs for employees by offering weekly prizes to those who sold the most.

Predictably, people resisted. Some told co-workers that they'd never join in.

But my friend persisted. In casual contacts and at every staff meeting she reminded people, "This is really important. And you'll benefit, not only if you win one of the weekly prizes, but also when we pass out bonuses at the end of the year." She conveyed this message in various forms, day in and day out, for a few months.

She praised those who joined in, and she especially praised those who had resisted at first but then made a few tentative sales.

She also made a big deal of each of the weekly prize winners, sending out a memo with the winner's name and accomplishments.

Before long, everybody was playing the game. It had sparked a competition among the group; each person now strove to sell the most. Though their efforts far outstripped the rewards, they all chose to do a good job for their boss, for themselves, and for the group. The program created a team spirit that had not existed before.

The keys to my friend's success: enthusiasm, the right program to motivate, and persistence in explaining its rewards and companywide benefits.

Listen

Good leaders listen.

They get their message across, then take input by asking questions like these:

- How are you doing?
- How can I help you?
- What stands in your way from achieving goals?
- How am I hindering you?
- How is the organization hindering you?
- What do you think of our goals and mission?
- What do you need that you don't have?
- Do you have a better way to achieve goals?
- Is the goal reasonable? If not, what would make it so?

To get good answers, people have to trust you. You won't earn trust if you:

—Take an answer and use it to club a person. ("What do you mean the goal is too hard to reach? If you and your crew didn't do things like miss milestones . . .")

—Use an answer to attack people at a later date.

—Make it seem that a "wrong" answer will end up in their personnel files.

You can still say no to a request, or redirect the thinking of your people. If someone says the goal is too ambitious, for instance, you can use it as a means to show your belief in him: "I know it seems tough to get all the orders out in one day, but I know you can do it. You and Johnny both have the experience and dedication to do it, and I'll be working on getting you the new software we need to expedite things. We can do it. I know we can."

Best Tip
Be approachable. Your people should feel they can come to you anytime with their concerns or suggestions.

Be sure not to brush off real concerns. Whatever you want done must be possible given time, energy, and a little luck.

Be Accessible

Good leaders are approachable. Even tough ones. You'll always have a few people afraid to talk to you about anything, but you'll find most people will interact given the chance and the knowledge that offering opinions won't hurt them.

You might set an explicit "open door" policy. One executive at ServiceMaster sets aside one entire Monday each month to receive employees, hear their concerns and ideas, and act upon them.

Symbolic acts help grease communication. Bill Arnold, one-time head of Columbia Centennial Medical Center in Tennessee, removed the door of his office.

His message: "You can come talk to me anytime." As an added

enticement, he kept a bowl of M&Ms on his desk.

The most time-honored way to be accessible is to wander around your realm. Find reasons to talk to people. Do it often enough and you'll earn their trust.

Celebrate and Praise Often

An important part of communicating values and goals is to reinforce them constantly. One way to do that is to praise those who act in accordance with them, or those who do extraordinary things in support of them. You can also hand out gift certificates, or little things like pens or refrigerator magnets emblazoned with a symbol that represents your department or company. Or you can celebrate.

I once worked at a start-up where we often celebrated reaching goals. We'd go out for dinner, or have after-work drinks, at the company's expense. At the event, we'd praise our people and each other, share credit, and tell stories about people going above and beyond the call of duty or acting in line with values. One such value was frugality; we heaped praise on whoever showed skill or resourcefulness in saving money.

| **Best Tip**
Put five pennies in your right pocket. Every time you praise a worker, put a penny in the left pocket. Aim to shift all the pennies by the end of the day.

These celebrations reinforced the idea that we were responsible for reaching goals and practicing values, and that good deeds were recognized and rewarded. They also allowed us to blow off a little steam so we didn't get burned out.

Don't Demean Workers

Watch what you call people. At Rosenbluth International, managers are called *leaders* and everyone else is an *associate*. Both words give employees a role to live up to.

It's common at some companies to call blue- or pink-collar

workers "hourlies." Not only does that demean, but it sets up a wall between managers and the non-salaried workers. I've even heard some managers call blue-collar workers "variable labor," referring to their status in the eyes of the plant accountant. It's no surprise when companies in which these terms are common have labor troubles.

Use the Right Words

You reinforce your mission, values, and goals with your language.

Bring up key words frequently in your conversations. For instance, "You know, if there's anything that keeps us from continuing to improve cycle time, I want to know about it."

Make up a handful of key words and use them at every chance. If a key value is speed, for instance, sprinkle words like *speed, fast, quick, rapid,* or *swift* into conversations. That reminds people— probably unconsciously—about what concerns you and what you'll be watching for.

Does it work? Motorola employees must be tired of hearing about Six Sigma, but they can't fail to know how important the concept is to the company and in the daily work they do.

Other good words, depending on your situation, include *productivity, innovation, service, merit, quality, teamwork, lean,* and *performance.* Just make sure you mean the words, and that they refer to concepts actually practiced by and rewarded in your organization or department.

The Agile Manager's Checklist

✔ Talk up your mission, values, and goals. Every day.
✔ Adopt a symbol that embodies goals or ideals.
✔ Listen!
✔ Celebrate when you reach major goals.

Every Employee a Leader

"If you don't understand that you work for your mislabeled 'subordinates,' then you know nothing of leadership. You know only tyranny."

DEE HOCK, A FORMER CEO, QUOTED IN *FAST COMPANY*

Chapter Seven

Managerial Practices That Create Leaders

Anita stopped the Agile Manager in the hallway.

"I want to tell you something," she said. "I was in the hospital visiting my grandmother yesterday evening. As I walked by the radiology lab, I saw a guy hunched down twiddling the dials on one of our analyzers. He seemed frustrated, so I introduced myself and told him that I had worked on that machine a few years ago.

"He said, 'I'm sure you're a nice person, but I hate this thing. Murphy Technology makes a better one—'" she saw the Agile Manager grimace "'—and I'm trying to get my boss to buy it.'

"So we talked a little bit about why, and I think he had some valid concerns. So you know what I did?"

"What? Tell me, tell me!"

"I invited him to visit us next Friday. I thought it would be useful if more of us understood his problems." She looked closely at the Agile Manager, not completely sure she'd done the right thing.

"Bravo! What a great idea. You get a gold star for initiative and quick thinking. Not only will we learn something, but maybe we can snatch a sale from Murphy."

"Well, I hope we don't try to sell him. I told him it would just be about that product and why he didn't like it."

"That's fine. What time? I want to make sure Buckley from marketing is there."

"12:30. It was the only time he could do it."

"Great—we'll have sandwiches and drinks. I'll see to it. Nice going Anita!"

If you've done a good job creating a motivating mission and setting challenging, achievable goals—with the input of people who must carry them out—you've done half the work. Your employees are on the road to feeling significant and excited about the present and future.

Yet there's still more to do.

Give People the Power to Handle Moments of Truth

You have great resources at your disposal that you may never have used. They are your people. They can contribute hugely to your mission—if you let them.

In his classic book *Moments of Truth*, former CEO Jan Carlzon of airline SAS defined a "moment of truth" as any time a customer came in contact with an SAS employee. Each such incident was where the company's mission, values, and strategies intersected with reality. SAS had, Carlzon figured, fifty million moments of truth each year, each lasting an average of fifteen seconds.

Moments of truth define the company for customers. And fifteen seconds isn't much. Carlzon realized that to improve customer service, while improving the leadership capabilities of his employees, he would have to give them the power they needed to manage customer interactions positively. He would have to prepare them to make decisions on the spot. He did, and SAS soared.

SAS and other companies know that the people closest to the customer have great power to define the customer's experience—for good or ill. One misstep, and a customer walks out of your life.

Likewise, you have great power to turn those who work for you into leaders. Give them the power to manage moments of truth. Train them, supply them with resources (especially information), and give them responsibility. They will surprise you.

Employees are like children waiting to be led only if we treat them like children. Treat them as adults and give them adult responsibilities, and you've got a company or department filled with leaders.

Give People Information

Once you've set strategies, standards, and goals, make sure people have the resources to do their jobs. That includes time, enough people, and money, primarily, but don't forget information.

In the words of Jan Carlzon, "An individual without information cannot take responsibility; an individual who is given information cannot help but take responsibility."

The days of information-hoarding are over. Competitive companies now share information freely with employees through computer networks. Networks can include information on:

- Company history and its current concerns;
- Competitors and the industry;
- Market data;
- Data on the broad economy;
- In-house tools and techniques;
- Company success stories (with lessons);
- On-call in-house experts in various areas;
- Who is working on what and with whom (projects database);
- Sales histories;
- Financial indicators and issues;
- Customers and vendors;
- Missions, values, and policies.

Generally, the more information the better. You never know when someone—at any level—will use it to advantage.

Offer Resources for Learning

The pace of change is greater than in the past, especially in technology-sensitive industries.

You've heard it before: People must now continue to learn throughout their working lives. In this age of teamwork and participation, for example, people need to learn how to work with one another. They need to learn to make good decisions so you don't have to. They need a methodology for identifying entrepreneurial opportunities and capitalizing upon them. They need to learn how to use the newest version of everyday software.

Best Tip

Share information—even sensitive financial data. Your people will feel more involved and make better decisions.

Sometimes they just need to know how to read. Motorola University teaches people to read and add numbers. At the same time, it teaches people the advanced skills Motorola needs to compete with other global giants like Mitsubishi or Nokia. If there's a business need for knowledge, Motorola U. teaches it.

OK, so you're not Motorola. What do you do? Send people to seminars. Pay their tuition for company-related courses. Hire trainers. Maintain a library and circulate business magazines.

Besides learning specific skills, your people need to understand your business and the industry. They need to understand how the company makes money (and how they benefit when it makes money). They need to understand their role in producing the goods and services people buy. If they do, they can make more intelligent decisions and plan their time better.

How could you teach that understanding? One way is to develop a class. Another, perhaps more dynamic way is to open up the organization so that people can spend time in different departments.

Also, you can make internal transfers easier, allow people to spend time in a department for an afternoon or a day, or allow "exchanges" in which people trade jobs for a few weeks or a month. And putting employees on the road with salespeople—or *as* salespeople—pays rich dividends.

Practice Servant-Leadership

While you have the right to expect excellent work and dedication from your people, they, in turn, have a right to expect good leadership. They must get the tools and support they need to do a good job—a reason for toiling hard, fair compensation, adequate resources, challenges to test and build their skills, and a constructive working environment.

> **Best Tip**
>
> Work to develop people. They'll repay you by saving their best efforts for you.

A concept coming into vogue, and with good reason, is "servant-leadership." That phrase is the brainchild of Robert Greenleaf, author, consultant, and a longtime manager at AT&T. (Greenleaf died in 1990.) In *The Servant as Leader*, Greenleaf wrote,

> It begins with the natural feeling that one wants to serve, to serve first. Then conscious choice brings one to aspire to lead. . . . The difference manifests itself in the care taken by the servant—first to make sure that other people's highest priority needs are being served.
>
> The best test, and difficult to administer, is: do those served grow as persons; do they, while being served, become healthier, wiser, freer, more autonomous, more likely themselves to become servants?

In developing people, you gain their commitment and loyalty. And they save their best efforts for you.

C. William Pollard, chairman of ServiceMaster, is the quintessential servant-leader. One of his guiding principles: The leader exists to improve the company. The company doesn't exist to improve the leader's life. And the key to improving the company is developing people.

Servant-leadership permeates ServiceMaster. Mere new-age mumbo jumbo? A $4 billion company, ServiceMaster's stockholders have enjoyed an average total annual return of more than 20 percent over the past twenty years. Not bad for a company managed by what some would consider "soft" ideas.

How to Serve Those You Lead

Following are ways you can keep people motivated, excited, and feeling important—all ingredients in a high-performance workplace. Together, these ideas will ensure that nothing stands between your people and the goals you've set for them.

Help develop employees. Offer training, send them to seminars, pay for classes. More important, offer on-the-job challenges. They teach just as well and the lessons burn deeper.

Help people achieve their goals. You have to know people well enough to know what their goals are. Don't assume you know; uncover them through casual conversation and through more formal events like appraisals.

Sometimes workers' goals are quite modest—a decent living, an interesting job, workplace camaraderie. You can satisfy them easily. Other times, goals are large. An ambitious employee, for example, may want to be CEO one day.

Good leaders don't fear the ambitious. They work to keep them focused on value-adding activities. But they also give them room to develop and advance, knowing that an ambitious person will go elsewhere otherwise.

If you create circumstances in which employees can achieve goals—especially by providing paths they can use to move up in the organization—you'll gain their long-term good will.

Create a trusting relationship. A cornerstone of trust, says leadership expert Michael Annison, is the sense that the leader is committed to something beyond his own well being. That something? Mission, values, and helping people improve.

Fight on their behalf. Get people the resources they need to do good work, even if you have to tussle with others in the organization to get it. And if someone at your level or above starts wondering about the value you and your people provide, trumpet that value so loud they back off.

Let them figure out how. Goals answer three questions: Who, what, and when. You—or your boss—has already figured out "why." You'll help motivate employees by letting them take care of the "how."

Some well-meaning over-controllers are way too intent on helping people figure out how to reach goals or meet standards. Offer guidance if asked, but be wary of interfering or doing the work yourself. You have better things to do.

Give people a role to live up to. Or, in the words of Dale Carnegie, "Give them a reputation to live up to." Rather than create a role of their own, many people wait for an authority figure—like a teacher or boss—to hand them one. Make it a good one.

Praise people for the traits you find most useful on the job, at the same time urging them on. For example: "You've really got a gift for numbers, Sally. I bet you could learn to use a spreadsheet program in no time. If you did that, I'm sure I could find some interesting work for you to do using it."

Another: "Tom, you have as much sales potential as anyone I've ever seen. I'd be surprised if you weren't one of the top ten salespeople in the company by the end of the year."

This technique can transform discipline problems, too. "Aggie, I know you want to do a good job for us. I know you have what it takes to turn out products free of defects. I know you want the company to do well so we can all do well . . ." Maybe Aggie knows none of these things, but you've given her some ideas to try on for size. Occasionally they stick.

Showing people you believe in them is sometimes enough to spur them to a higher level of productivity.

Make every job important. In some companies, there are no low-level jobs. FedEx drivers, for example, get extensive training in using the latest technology to track packages and provide information to customers. They are also trained to sell FedEx services (and get a bonus every time they create a customer). The training and responsibility give them power, the will to excel, and the ability to manage moments of truth in ways that benefit the company.

Not only are employees more productive after this training, but they understand they are responsible for much more than delivering packages. They are responsible for the success of the company.

|Best Tip

Hire people from diverse backgrounds. You'll get a multiplicity of views, which is essential in deciding how to proceed in today's markets.

Promote diversity. Many different viewpoints combine to create a strong, resilient group.

Include people in your decisions. If you want wholehearted support for your decisions, get input from the people who will be affected. That's standard operating practice at Motorola.

It will be easier for them to accept difficult decisions if they've had a chance to speak their minds. People want to be heard, and listening to their ideas shows respect for their intelligence and concern for their daily work life.

Besides, you'll be surprised frequently—people might have better solutions to problems than those you've considered. When Bill Arnold, former head of Columbia Centennial Medical Center, was planning a new building, he solicited the input of janitors. He figured they could help create a design for a building that's easier to maintain and clean. They did.

Support those who fail or need help. Everybody deserves a chance. If you give people a few chances, and they fail, don't write them off. Show respect by working with them to get a few wins that may spark a turnaround.

I was once in charge of a salesman who would come back with daily sales half or less of what another person would bring in. My first reaction was anger. But I made that anger productive by going out on the road with him a few times. I soon saw it wasn't a matter of poor technique or a lack of confidence in the products. He was timid, and he needed an example of how to stride into a store forthrightly and with great confidence. Within a year, that salesman was setting records.

Best Tip

Delegate. There's no better way to take a load off yourself and get people to think like a boss.

Delegate. Nothing gets people thinking like a boss, and feeling important, better than delegation. Delegated work is, by definition, higher-level work than an employee is used to doing. Delegation builds confidence, and it helps employees acquire skills, experience, and insight. Best of all, it frees you to lead.

Here are five simple guidelines for delegating:

1. When you delegate a job, give it to the lowest-level person who can handle it. It'll be more of a challenge for that person, and the work is done by the least-costly staffer.

2. Tell the person, explicitly, the result you want. "I need a flawless report that analyzes the Mexican market for machine tooling. It should offer hard numbers concerning the size of the market and the share held by our competitors, and it should recommend whether we should get into it or not."

3. Don't tell the person how to obtain the result. If you do, the person will naturally assume that you want the work done a certain way, and she'll ask, repeatedly, what to do next. Merely tell her you are available for guidance, but you'd prefer that she figure out how to do the job done on her own. If you pick the right person for the job, you will be surprised at the creativity she brings to it.

4. If you check up at all, do it unobtrusively and infrequently. "How's it going?" should suffice.

5. Never take a delegated job back. Poor managers often do this, unable to relinquish control. Another problem: Employees,

skillful in shunting off responsibility, hand jobs back. Don't let them.

Hold people accountable. You do people honor when you expect them to meet their obligations. You are saying, "You are adults. You can handle these responsibilities." If they fail at a job or task, send them back to do it again. If they are not up to the work you've given them, give them a new job or let them go. If you fail to hold people accountable, you fail as a leader. Your results will suffer, and some people will take advantage of you.

Never ask anyone to do something you wouldn't do. Part of the job of any retailer is to check up on the competition. David Glass, CEO of Wal-Mart, is willing to do just what he asks his people to do. He roams the aisles of other retailers, tape recorder in hand, at the risk of getting kicked out. Sometimes he does. And it's hard to maintain your dignity when you get kicked out of a store. Especially when you're a high-profile CEO of a prominent company.

Be prepared to do the dirty work along with your people. You'll gain their respect.

The Agile Manager's Checklist

✔ Give your employees the power to handle "moments of truth" with customers.

✔ Provide people with more information than you think is necessary.

✔ Encourage people to acquire new skills.

✔ Help your people achieve their goals. They'll show their gratitude in numerous ways.

✔ Get input from people affected by your decisions.

Chapter Eight

Organizational Structures That Create Leaders

"I don't care what your job description is, Carlos. I don't remember why I even gave you the title 'Product Design Consultant.' I probably thought it might make you feel good about your work. The point is, you're on the product-development team—with me, Wanda, Tony, Phil, William, Myoshi, Anita, Ted, and everyone else. Our job, together, is to create salable products."

The Agile Manager stopped to catch his breath and see if Carlos, six months out of college, had anything to say. Carlos bit his lip, so the Agile Manager continued.

"The one thing I hate to hear is 'It's not my job.' It's a cliché—people only say it as a joke."

"I meant it as a joke, too," said Carlos.

"But you wouldn't drive the design over to Everett Engineering on your way home. We lost a day. And we spent $35 on a courier." The Agile Manager paused.

"I'm sorry," said Carlos, looking down.

"Carlos, believe it or not, I'm not disciplining you," the Agile Manager said warming up his tone. "I just want you to understand that all of us do what's necessary to produce great products. Sometimes that means doing work of the highest order, sometimes it *means doing scut work. Sometimes it means doing work that is outside of your regular duties." Carlos nodded.*

"Now, I'm late for a meeting and I'd like you to help me out. Would you please go over to R&D and ask John for the preliminary research results on how well the new motor stands up to heavy use? Ask him to go through the test process with you so you can let me know what he did."

"Sure, but don't I have to go to his boss?" Carlos seemed happy but bewildered.

"No. Debbie and I have an understanding that our people can avoid normal channels for routine stuff. It speeds things up."

"Oh," said Carlos. "And, um, am I in trouble?"

"You? You're the best Product Design Consultant I have. Now go and do good."

Carlos smiled and left.

Your organization must be set up to deliver on the mission. Ideally, nothing gets in the way of the work you do for customers.

For example, many companies organize in a way that benefits themselves, rather than customers or the market.

Though it's getting more rare, you can still hear managers say things like, "We can't let customers tell us how to run our business." That's a sure sign that a barrier exists between an organization and its mission. It also suggests an arrogance that may come back to haunt the company.

The rest of this chapter will give you some ideas on ways to remove impediments to performance.

Decentralize

One way companies are doing a better job serving customers and achieving the mission is to decentralize. An article in the February 1997 issue of *Fast Company* describes SOL, a Finnish cleaning-services company. SOL has decentralized by letting its 135 supervisors lead their own teams. These teams do their own budgets, hire, set goals, make deals with customers and more. If they want, they can set up in their own offices. Teams, further, set higher performance goals than senior managers would, and they meet them.

Small units generally live or die using their wits to get the job done properly while remaining accountable for meeting goals. Decentralization thus turns employees into leaders. Can you imagine how long it takes a new SOL worker to figure out that it's his or her job to satisfy customers? Probably about five minutes. It is, for the right kind of employee, exhilarating to have a chance to perform with little interference.

Use Teamwork

Like SOL, many companies have turned to teamwork to get things done. In blue-collar settings, these can be permanent, self-directed work teams. In white-collar environments, these tend to be project teams that form to solve specific problems or develop a specific opportunity. With the mission completed, teams disband.

In most cases, team members are still attached to particular functions, like marketing, manufacturing, or finance. They report to bosses in their areas. But the company has made it easy for people from different areas to join forces and get work done without disturbing their normal tasks or threatening the boss's authority.

At Cypress Semiconductor, for example, teams meet and set goals. These goals, however, are subject to the approval of functional managers, who may want their people to reprioritize work.

Good teamwork takes certain skills and some trial-and-error experience, but it can be done. At the very least, plan to train people in team and meeting skills before instituting any such program.

Get Rid of Disabling Bureaucracy and Hierarchy

Multiple levels of authority get in the way of your mission. Hierarchy slows things down and promotes a committee attitude in which no one sticks his or her neck out. Also, hierarchy hampers leadership. People wait for orders rather than initiating action, and they don't take responsibility.

If it's in your power, reduce the number of management levels to the point that people can act with a measure of autonomy while maintaining accountability.

Decentralize wherever you can. It turns employees into leaders.

While you're at it, break down the bureaucracy. Most large companies still have too many staffers interfering in the work of people who do the work that pays the bills. At the very least, make sure support staff knows that its customers are those on the front lines.

Set Up Entrepreneurial Units

Creating entrepreneurial units, or permitting their creation, is the ultimate in promoting leadership skills in all of an organization's employees.

Why encourage entrepreneurship? Entrepreneurial units are likely to stick closer to their mission and customers and make leaders of its employees.

Many companies have told internal services, "You're on your own. If you make it, great. If you don't, you're out of work." For example, General Electric told its manufacturing units that it could use GE's R&D departments, or they could go outside the company. That changed the viewpoint of GE's R&D people, who realized they had better serve the customer—or plan to find other work.

Similarly, companies pit outside vendors against their computer service, human resources, and advertising departments. Inhuman? Hardly. It's more inhuman to force employees to use monopolistic services if they could get work done better and cheaper elsewhere.

Author and consultant Gifford Pinchot believes that allowing internal competition is the only way to light a fire under inefficient service providers. It does no good, he maintains, to try to train people to be entrepreneurial or more productive.

What if the old Soviet Union, he wonders, had simply tried to teach state-run monopolies to take more risks or be more responsive to customers? Would they have succeeded in learning those skills? Of course not. Learning to become market-oriented could happen only one way—by removing monopoly status.

*B*est *Tip*
Make sure everyone has an e-mail account. Some consider it a time-waster, but it's revolutionized the transfer of information. And for the better.

Some companies, especially smaller ones, encourage spin-offs if a person or a small team has what it considers a marketable idea. The parent company can keep a small stake and let the spin-off loose, or it can keep a larger stake and keep the new company under its wing (and control), offering capital, support, guidance, and other benefits.

Make Entrepreneurship Part of the Job

You can promote entrepreneurship without turning people loose to run their own units. Help people focus on satisfying new or existing markets with innovations.

There are several ways to encourage entrepreneurship at an organizational level. As mentioned, 3M allows technical people to use 15 percent of their time on projects of their own choosing. Perhaps more important, 3M expects 30 percent of its revenue to come from products four years old or younger. As a result of such policies, 3M pumps out a prodigious number of products—five hundred in 1996 alone.

DuPont and Motorola both have been known to yank revenue-producing, but mature, products from the market. That forces certain departments or divisions to replace revenues, which keeps minds focused on taking risks.

Any such practice signals to people that new product or service ideas are not only appreciated but expected. It imposes discipline, which ignites creativity and innovation. And it ignites leadership in the process, because people realize they have to produce. Their jobs depend on it.

Encourage Porous Boundaries

Departments with thin walls allow information to flow in and out. It gets to whoever needs it sooner, and it stands a better chance of remaining unfiltered or unaltered.

Interesting things happen when people at opposite ends of the business can exchange ideas. Innovations emerge, efficiencies multiply, service improves, and new markets are uncovered. Things happen faster.

E-mail has probably done more to remove barriers between departments and functions than anything else. Project teams run a close second. Both do a great job weaving ties among departments. People get to know each other and understand how they can help one another succeed.

A true "boundaryless" company (a term originated at General Electric) doesn't stop at department walls—it allows people from different companies to mingle. Many companies, for example, now have employees stationed at key vendor or customer sites—permanently.

Leaders in boundaryless organizations don't relinquish power. They still keep a keen eye on what's happening, and they remain responsible for results. But unlike the old days, they trust more people to operate like leaders to improve results.

Make Job Titles Flimsy

It used to be that you were your job title. It still means that in some traditional companies, and it still means that where unions have iron-clad work rules.

But in many more places than before, titles and job descriptions are loosening. Fewer people have flunky-level titles like "assistant" or "secretary." People now have titles like "coordinator" or "specialists in business development."

Some lament the passing of meaningful titles. I don't. The ultimate end of this trend can already be seen at the new movie studio, SKG Dreamworks. There, nobody has a title. That makes things interesting and ambiguous. And out of ambiguity rises innovation.

Flimsy job titles and descriptions also encourage a team attitude. If no one has a job set in concrete, no one can say, "I don't do that kind of work." If something needs to be done, the person closest at hand does it. Even the leader. Loose titles force the focus where it should be—on doing the work that people pay the organization to do.

Set Up Informal Mentoring Programs

People start to learn when they have to teach.

Begin an informal mentoring program in which new employees are paired with older ones. The veterans can help train, offer counseling, become a shoulder to cry on, and provide insights on "the way things work around here." Give it a set length, like three months. If the pair continues informally, great.

Teaching brings out the idealism in people. They want to show new people their best sides, so they'll usually set cynicism or hostility aside. Besides getting new employees up to speed faster, the veterans will surprise themselves with the insights they come up with. They'll grow, and grow more valuable to you.

The Agile Manager's Checklist

✔ Set up your organization to deliver on the mission.
✔ To promote efficiency, create entrepreneurial units.
✔ Make job titles flimsy enough so people don't feel confined by them.

Chapter Nine

Lead—But Manage Well

The Agile Manager sat in front of his computer screen playing with numbers. He had devised a few measures that seemed to reflect success in his department—and that could signal danger on the horizon.

One measure he called "innovations per employee." He defined innovation loosely but kept it focused on products rather than processes. (He had a separate measure for process improvements.) To him, an innovation was a new product or an enhancement of an old one. He also included new parts or components designed in-house.

Right now the figure was 17.6 innovations per year per employee. That's a far cry from the first year he tracked it—9.3—but not as good as three years ago, when it hit 19.1.

Of course, he thought, I've added three people since then. Still, why add a person if it doesn't help you jack up the number of innovations? The measure had helped in his hiring, too. Could this person, he asked himself, directly help crank out more new products, or better ones?

The Agile Manager wasn't entirely happy with his measure of innovations. It wasn't always easy to know when to call something an innovation, and it was too tempting to call a minor change an *innovation. He found it difficult to be consistent in applying the definition.*

That's why he also kept track of "harder" ratios like employee turnover (always very low) and sales per employee in his department.

Sales per employee was a proxy measure, because the company had many more people than those in his department.

To arrive at it, he took total revenue and subtracted the sales of services and any other income not related to the products his department developed. He updated it quarterly when the company released sales figures.

The Agile Manager gazed at the sales-per-employee chart on his screen and smiled. Ever upward, he thought. That's one trend I don't want to mess with. I think I'll print this out and put it on the bulletin board. If I'm lucky, the boss will wander by and see it.

Some experts on leadership disparage what they consider mere management. Managers, they say, are too interested in controlling people and things, they watch budgets and the bottom line too carefully, and they are overly concerned with the short-term.

I've never understood this view. An organization, for example, absolutely must have good systems, which by nature control. It must be as mindful of the short term as of the long term. It must, at times, direct and redirect people. And if someone, somewhere, is not tracking budgets and financial results—watch out.

Some of the worst leaders practice idealistic leadership at the expense of good management. They are all vision and values, long-term views and goals. They show little concern for doing the daily work of the company or department. Ideas excite them more than honing the operations that support the mission.

A friend of mine once had a boss who could see only the forest, and not the trees in it. He brought the nonprofit organization he led to the brink of disaster a number of times. His main flaw: He involved the organization in long-term, mission-supporting programs, but without stopping to consider how he'd pay for them. Good financial management would have saved his neck any number of times.

Worse, he never attended to details. He'd let things slide—bills, legal and tax issues—until they got the organization into trouble. He considered details beneath him. Good management, however, focuses on details—on the "how" of anything.

"Leaders" like these wreck companies and departments. They waste good resources, including people.

Management Skills Leaders Need

Here's a short list of the management skills any good leader should have. If you don't have a skill or the desire to acquire it, make sure one of your people does. It's worth the effort. Good management skills, in combination with the leadership skills this book describes, creates something relatively rare—a visionary who gets things done.

Best Tip

Learn to read balance sheets and calculate financial ratios as well as an accountant. It's rocket fuel for your career.

Understand finances. Numbers are another language that describe what you are doing. They provide an advantage—they boil down your acts in a way that lets you know whether they are feasible or not, and whether you are getting results, or not.

Money should never be the sole focus of what you do, but recognize that it's organizational blood.

Learn to budget and read financial statements. Budget responsibly by zero-basing your estimates. That means don't take last year's budget and add 3 percent per category. Visit each category anew to decide what level is appropriate. Sometimes that level is zero.

Learn to read income and cash-flow statements, and the balance sheet. They reveal things about your department or company people sometimes don't want to talk about.

Develop operational skills. It's up to you to see that operations don't interfere with pursuing your mission. Operations, in fact, should make it easier to fulfill the mission.

Investigate all your business practices and processes. Map them out and work constantly to make them more efficient and to eliminate blockages that impede the flow.

Make good decisions. Experienced leaders tend to make intuitive decisions. But they do so based on years of analysis and learning. Inexperienced leaders who make gut decisions end up sorry. Take the time to gather information, investigate options, and think through the possible results of any course you take. Balance intuition with analysis.

Keep people focused. A good mission and concrete, challenging goals are the best way to keep people focused. Sometimes, however, you need to lean on people who aren't performing. They could range from nonstop talkers, for example, to those not up to the challenge at hand. Don't let non-performers slide. Deal with them.

Watch key measures. Your business or department has key numbers that bear watching. If you head the company, they may be profitability ratios, sales figures, or companywide efficiency ratios. If you head a department, a key measure could be inventory turnover, collection period, transactions per day, sales per employee, value-added per employee, cycle time, or any of a hundred other measures.

Best Tip
Figure out which measures—sales, transactions, etc.—best reflect the success of your department. Then watch them diligently.

Figure out which ones are key to your success. Start tracking and improving them and don't stop until you find a better measure.

Set productivity-improvement goals. One of your goals, whether you are a company chief or department head, should be to do more with the same amount of resources, year in and year out. A good leader will demand that, knowing that productivity improvements underlie success—not to mention improved salary and benefits for employees.

Any productivity measure relates output to input. Perhaps your key measure is already a productivity measure—transactions per employee, or sales or profits per employee. Analyze what you do in your department, focusing on the things you can count. Then figure what resources, in terms of supplies, people, equipment, and money, it takes to do it. Aim to improve output a little more every year—in the range of 3 to 5 percent—using the same amount of resources.

Best Tip

Set regular appointments with yourself to plan for the future.

When tracking quantities of transactions, keep results in mind. Busyness is not necessarily productive. If you do market research, for example, tracking the number of focus groups conducted doesn't serve much purpose. Instead, think in terms of results delivered to customers—worthwhile studies completed, problems solved per employee, error-free orders entered, packages shipped on time, etc.

Productivity measures spur creative thinking. How will you increase output? Buy a new machine? Hire another person? Make work processes more efficient? Figuring out the answers is what good management is all about.

Train well. Good training is a management issue. If you train well, you can eliminate problems down the road.

Any time you change operating procedures or expect people to do new things, set aside the time to train them to do the work properly.

Plan. Take the time to plan how you will execute your mission. Look ahead three months, six months, one year, and three years. What pitfalls do you see? Opportunities? Trends that may affect your work? Competition from new sources? What kind of resources will you need months and years hence?

You won't be able to answer most of these questions accurately, and some perhaps not at all. The important thing is to scan the horizon and plot how you'll reach your destination. As any sailor knows, navigation is a full-time job.

Many managers say they don't have time to plan. Make time—it's among your most potent labor-saving activities.

Analyze your mission every so often. Some dreamers get so enamored of the vision that they don't see a better opportunity come along, or they refuse to acknowledge that things aren't working out. Don't fall in love with your mission or vision. Once you've created it, turn a cold, detached eye on it occasionally.

Buy the best equipment and technology. Technology makes people more productive. Spend liberally on machinery, computers, cell phones, and anything else that can help people work faster, more accurately or efficiently, and with greater ease.

Some managers don't see how expensive it is not to invest in technology. They may have one old printer hooked up to a local area network. People waste time waiting for their jobs to print, or waiting for a repair person. And a slow printer becomes like the water cooler—a place where people congregate to socialize when maybe they should be working.

The Agile Manager's Checklist

✔ Investigate your business practices and processes. Then work to optimize them.
✔ In making decisions, balance intuition with analysis.
✔ Set productivity improvement goals yearly.
✔ Train well. It eliminates problems.
✔ Don't skimp. Buy the best technology.

Chapter Ten

Lead Change Gracefully

"I was just thinking," said the Agile Manager as he twirled the phone cord. "When we succeed in getting development lead time down to 120 days, we could turn what we've learned into a seminar for others in the company. Or teach anyone who wanted to learn. Disney holds seminars to teach what they know about managing people. It's a pretty big business for them."

"Sounds great," said his boss. "But let's get to 120 days before we print up the brochures. Where are we now?"

"Right around three months. We've cut three months off."

"Fantastic. Keep at it."

Just as the Agile Manager hung up, Wanda came in.

"You know, Wanda, I have this great idea. We get down to 120 days and we turn our learning into a teaching module for those in the company. Then we sell seminars to other companies."

"What, and teach our competitors everything we've learned?"

"We wouldn't let 'em know everything. We'd keep the good stuff to ourselves. What do you think?"

"I think," said Wanda, "that shaving that last month off the lead time is going to be hell. We've done all the easy stuff. We've also done all the medium-hard stuff. I don't know how we're going to do the rest."

"Oh, we'll do it all right," said the Agile Manager. "I'll sleep in the office if I have to. One day soon we'll get down to 120 days, and then we'll be pumping products out of here like crazy. We'll be like Sony or Mitsubishi or whoever it is that introduces three new products every day. Development costs are low enough that they can do market testing with real products. Won't it be great when we get to that point?"

Wanda never failed to be amazed by this man's optimism. People who don't know firsthand how smart he is must think he's a moron, she thought.

Wanda let down her iron overcoat briefly. "It will be," she said, blessing him with a rare smile that vanished quickly. "But look, I have more pressing problems. First . . ."

In a sense, this whole book has been about leading change. Business *is* change.

Judging by the current literature, you'd think people had discovered change in just the past five years or so. What have people been doing for the past few thousand years?

Still, there are times when you want to stop what you're doing, and start doing something new. And you want people to know that you're breaking with the past to start afresh.

Typical change situations include:

- Restructuring your business or department to serve customers better;
- Reengineering a process or changing an operational practice;
- Installing a program like just-in-time inventory replenishment or total quality management;
- Closing down part of your business and laying people off or putting them elsewhere;
- Initiating a companywide cost-cutting program;
- Changing to a project-team structure.

Leading a change effort requires all the skills already mentioned in this book—and more.

You Can't Make People Change

First understand that you can't make people do anything unless you point a gun at them. A real one. People do what they want to do. If you try to force change, you'll fail. Period. People will resist you with all their might.

That's why your job is to lead people to decide to change their behavior. Through a combination of logic, emotion, and your best human-relations and communication skills, you show them that it's in their interest to change. You show—at every step of the way—

Best Tip

Lead people into change. Forcing them doesn't work and never will.

what's in it for them. Leading change is a sales job.

Don't sell, however, at the expense of listening. People resisting change sometimes have good reasons for doing so. Find out what they are.

When you make your pitch, tie the benefits directly to each individual: You'll save your job. You'll get paid more. You'll learn new skills that will make you more valuable to us or anyone else. You'll ensure this company remains healthy for the next fifty years.

Be as persuasive as you can, but never lie. During periods of change, trust is of paramount importance.

Have a Double Vision

Visions aren't always required in business. In change efforts, they are.

People may be complacent and happy. They wonder why you are causing so much fuss. And if they aren't happy—they know, for instance, that the company is in trouble—they may be scared.

It's your job to tell them what the problem or challenge is, and why the company or department needs to change.

You need two visions. Your first vision is a dark one. It describes what will happen if you don't change. For example: "If we don't change to a just-in-time inventory supply system, we'll lose a lot of business, and many of you will lose your jobs. Brown Auto has already told us we have to start shipping just-in-time by July 1 or they'll switch suppliers. National is giving us until February 1 of next year. Five or six other companies are starting to talk to us about it. If we don't change, I think we might be out of business. And not in five years, but next year. The situation is that dire."

After painting the dark picture, follow up with a bright, enticing vision. "I think changing to a JIT system is gonna make this a great company. I look ahead and this is what I see: We're working in a team system with the best and newest equipment, we're doing more business with existing accounts, we're picking up new ones—we're ready, in short, for whatever the new century brings. And not only do we have our jobs, but they pay better and they'll be more fun. We'll all have new skills and more reason to use our brains on the job."

A vision for a change effort needn't be of the change-the-world variety, although it can be. It can be more about saving jobs, having more fun, and increasing business with benefits for all.

A good vision is understandable and compelling. It makes people willing to sacrifice today for a better tomorrow. That sacrifice includes disruption, extra time spent learning, or perhaps picking up the pieces after a downsizing. Make sure, therefore, you pay attention to the benefits in terms of skills learned, capabilities enhanced, new business found, and compensation improved.

Finally, a good vision for change has a point, and usually a financial one. You're not changing over to a team system for the fun of it, for example, but because you expect it to improve productivity by 5 percent a year.

Get Specific

Visions are great but, as always, you must take your head out of the clouds and get down to ground level—how daily work will change.

"So that's my vision of our department after we move to just-in-time delivery. What do we need to do to make it a reality? We'll go through two major changes. First, we're changing over to a self-directed team system. What that means is [x, y, and z]. And don't worry—you're going to get all the training you need. Second, we'll be changing how we handle inventory from top to bottom. For example . . ."

Work with Tradition

One reason change efforts fail is that you have to contend with history. If your company has been around for a hundred years, employees may figure that it's been doing things right. Why change?

Or, your effort to change might seem to go against the philosophy of a beloved founder. "Mr. Jones wouldn't have tried something like this," people may whisper.

Acknowledge the past. And be sure to point out that the company has been in business for a hundred years precisely because it has embraced change. Give examples. "When Mr. Jones saw that telegraph was dying, he abandoned any new investment in it and opened the state's first local telephone company. People thought he was nuts, but . . ."

Use Values as Guides

When changing, don't change or contradict the company's core ethical values.

Values should persist through changes. They are often the most permanent elements of a company—and stronger than steel or bricks.

Johnson & Johnson's credo, for example, represents bedrock values: "We believe our first responsibility is to the doctors, nurses and patients, to mothers and fathers and all others who use our products. . . . We are responsible to our employees, the men and women who work with us throughout the world. Everyone must be considered as an individual. We must respect their dignity and recognize their merit. . . ."

No matter what businesses J&J gets into, no matter how it changes, employees know it will never abandon its credo. That's a mighty potent security blanket for those going through change.

Create a Sense of Urgency

It's hard to get people to change when they see no reason to. If the company is doing well, and they feel good about their work and how they pursue it, they may think you're an idiot for suggesting change.

Your request for change must be saturated with urgency, otherwise people will take their time to come around to your point of view—if they ever do.

Sometimes this is easy. If your company is sinking deeper into the mud with each passing day, it's not hard to keep up the daily drumbeat for change and have people believe in the need for it.

But what if the crisis is months or a year off? Create a looming crisis you can point to as the reason for change:

"You look around you and see that things appear to be normal. I can tell you they're not. We've been managing this production line the same way for the last twenty years. A lot has happened since then. Our competitors—Acme in particular—have been upgrading their capabilities and investing in new equipment at a furious pace. We could wake up one day a year from now and discover that a quarter of our business is walking out the door . . ."

You can also create a sense of urgency by showing people how your present practices have kept you from opportunity. "You know, a Japanese company scoping out potential vendors came to visit us two months ago. They were impressed with the operation. They especially liked our team system. To them, that was a good sign. But when we started talking about the equipment we use to ensure quality, things got a bit shaky. And when they found out our defect rates, they ended the meeting. That's the last we heard of them. I don't need to tell you that a large chunk of business fell through our fingers."

Get a Few Early Wins

People will be skeptical of you and your plans. Show them you mean business—and that you have good ideas—by getting results quickly.

Practically speaking, that means breaking down your change effort into a few manageable chunks. If you know you have to revamp order fulfillment from top to bottom, for instance, concentrate your efforts on the front or back end, and shave time or gain

Best Tip

Show people how the status quo has kept you from an opportunity. It's a powerful argument for change.

efficiencies there. Then move on to the next challenge. With a few wins under your belt, the job becomes slightly easier.

Perform Symbolic Acts

Smart leaders trying to get a message across resort to drama. They destroy a piece of equipment, burn an old policy manual, or sell off assets.

The first thing Al Dunlap did when he came in to turn around Scott paper was sell its three-building "campus" in Philadelphia. He moved headquarters to Florida. It was his way of saying, "everything is different now." (Plus, he needed the money. The buildings brought in $39 million.)

Don't do anything employees would consider heresy—like tear up a picture of a former leader—but be ready to sacrifice a symbol of the old way to signal a new day for all.

A potent symbolic (and practical) act? Get rid of people who continue to work against you.

Share Information

Don't withhold information that affects employees. If you do, you'll destroy trust. For example, if you know jobs will be cut but don't tell people until the day you ax them, you'll lose respect.

In a situation like that, say, in the beginning, "Some of you will probably lose your jobs. I'll do my best to find out who is likely to be affected and when." Then fulfill your promise.

Share any information regarding the change you can. If you're changing a process, make process maps available. Introduce people to those working on the project and make them available periodically to discuss progress. If reports or memos shed light, pass them around. You can't offer too much information. You want to keep their heads filled with facts, not baseless rumors.

> **Best Tip**
>
> Create measures that show you're making progress. Post results regularly for all to see.

I once worked for a company that moved to a new location, changing operational procedures at the same time. It did a masterful job keeping people apprised of what was happening and when. It showed plans and designs, asked for input, took people on site visits to show them where they would be, and in general made the change as painless as possible.

People looked forward to the move, even though it would add twenty minutes to the commute for most of them.

Measure Your Progress

You're asking people to go from here to there. Where, exactly is "there"? How will you know when you reach it? By tracking relevant indicators and measures.

If you're doing a reengineering project, for example, you'll focus on something like how long it takes to complete a cycle, a transaction, fulfillment, or product development. So you say: "Right now it takes us a full year to develop a product. We won't rest until we get that figure down to six months." Or, "It takes eight days to process an application. Of that time, people are working on it—adding value—for twelve hours. With training and new technology, we think we can get the total processing time down to one day, and value-adding time to six hours."

In changing processes, you may have to dig into them deeply and come up with measures pertaining to its parts—how fast some activities are done, how long product sits at each stage, or how much backlog exists.

If you're restructuring or cutting costs, you'll focus on return on equity, cash flow, or indicators like profit or sales per employee.

If you're increasing production by instituting flexible manufacturing methods, watch for an increase in products produced, unit costs lowered, and perhaps better quality.

If you're installing a program like TQM, you should see results in fewer defects or fewer warranty claims or returns.

Don't forget indicators that highlight the big picture. Are you gaining market share? Is morale higher? Are customers satisfied?

Don't Be Afraid to Lead

When your company or department is in trouble, take charge. People are probably thirsting for real leadership. Move boldly to enact the changes you know are necessary. Your people will make way for you and your ideas.

The Agile Manager's Checklist

✔ In a change situation, create two visions—one that shows what happens if you don't change, and one that shows what happens if you do.

✔ Work with tradition. Your job is hard enough without going against the grain.

✔ Keep your values in mind as you lead change.